P9-DEV-967

Amos among the Prophets

Composition and Theology

ROBERT B. COOTE

ᖴ FORTRESS PRESS   Philadelphia

The quotation on pages 29–31 is from Eric R. Wolf, *Peasants*, ©
1966, pp. 55–56. Reprinted by permission of Prentice Hall, Inc.,
Englewood Cliffs, N.J.

COPYRIGHT © 1981 BY FORTRESS PRESS

All rights reserved. No part of this publication may be reproduced,
stored in a retrieval system, or transmitted, in any form or by any
means, electronic, mechanical, photocopying, recording or otherwise, without the prior permission of the copyright owner.

Library of Congress Cataloging in Publication Data

Coote, Robert B   1944–
   Amos among the Prophets.

   Bibliography: p.
     1. Bible. O.T. Amos—Criticism, interpreta-
tion, etc. 2. Amos, the prophet. I. Title.
BS1585.2.C66   224′.806   80–8054
ISBN 0–8006–1400–3

8268F80   Printed in the United States of America   1–1400

Contents

Preface

This book is meant for ministers and intermediate seminary students. I hope scholars may also benefit from it.

My debt to specialists is enormous. The works listed in the section "For Further Reading" are some I have found particularly helpful. Many of them are referred to by author in the main discussion.

I am grateful to my family and to the score of colleagues, students, and staff who have assisted me. I want to record my special thanks to Marvin Chaney and Marilyn Chilcote for their contributions to the way I think and express myself in this book.

I remain in doubt whether God should ever pardon a person for writing a book about a book. For the present I must be content with the ghost of a pardon tokened by the many friends who have gone ahead and helped me write this book. They have done so fully aware they would someday sit down to read or reread it and get up after a few hours in doubt whether God should pardon a person for reading a book about a book. If by chance there is no pardon, I will be content with their company—and glad for yours.

1

Three Stages of Composition

Prophecy comes in spurts. That's why reading a book like Amos is different from reading a book like Genesis, Mark, or Romans. Amos has too little story, too little train of thought, and too little internal coherence to hold interest for more than a few verses or, at most, a chapter. Prophecy originated in spurts, it is printed in spurts, and if we grasp for the meaning to be gotten from one of these spurts, we are being true to its origin and essential character.

Circumstances make it difficult to take prophecy more than a bit at a time, anyway. Not many people have much time when they get around to reading the Bible. Even the professionals are likely to be looking mainly for a springboard for a sermon. Preachers settle for short passages because that's the custom or because the lectionary tells them to. The commentaries they may refer to isolate short sections for in-depth treatment. Devotional helps use prophecy as though it were shampoo—a little is supposed to go a long way. The New Testament schools us to take prophecy one short segment at a time. If anyone should follow a recent trend and try to read longer sections, he or she may become discouraged by the hodgepodge after only a page or two, or frustrated by the difficulty of relating a particular passage from Amos, say, to a commentator's discussion of Amos as a whole.

Prophecy comes in spurts, and for many reasons we read it that way. But prophecy also comes strung together, and that is the reason for this book. Prophecy comes, for instance, in the book of Amos. The prophetic spurt is a challenging item, no question. I know its excitement. But I have had two other experiences that I think are also important: first, I have found other meanings in longer sections of prophecy, up to an entire book, and even more. Second, I have often understood a single prophetic oracle better when I could read it in the context of the longer section or strand of which it is a part. One purpose of this book is to help you enrich your understanding of prophecy by reading longer sections of it.

Perhaps the most important reason longer sections of prophecy are difficult to get hold of and deal with is that they are the result of a lengthy and complex process of composition. To understand longer sections of prophecy, it is necessary to understand this process of composition. The "catchword" principle, which suggests that the oracles are for the most part linked haphazardly by similar sounds, words, and phrases, is no longer a sufficient explanation. This is not a new insight in biblical study, but so far it has required critical subtlety, involved considerable scholarly disagreement, and lacked any bearing on us as persons. Without necessarily settling the scholarly debate, in this book I want to describe the process of composition in such a way that you can see how it works and why it is important.

Although I am going to talk mainly about the book of Amos, what I say applies to other prophetic books, too, when appropriately adapted. I have chosen the book of Amos as my example for four reasons: (1) it is short; (2) though Amos is by no means the original prophet, his oracles are among the earliest contained in the documents that came to be written prophecy; (3) the growth of the book of Amos is clearer at present than that of other prophetic books, with the possible exception of Micah; and (4) the Hebrew text of the book of Amos is comparatively free of corruption. It is important to remember that Amos is just an example. To understand the process by which the book of Amos came to be is to learn an approach that will be useful with *all* prophetic literature.

In its present form the book of Amos was written by more than one author at more than one time. Like almost all the prophetic books, it is the end result of a series of recompositions of the original words of a named prophet. Many of the words in the book of Amos were composed in roughly their

present form by Amos in the third quarter of the eighth ①
century. In between Amos and the final edition of the book
of Amos there were other editions of his words, possibly sev-②
eral, composed by several different authors. In order to sim-
plify, and without overly distorting the evidence, I am going
to treat these intervening editions as though there were only
one of them. Then the book as we have it was composed by a
final author sometime near the end of the Babylonian exile or ③
shortly thereafter. Thus I talk about a *three-stage process*.
The main purpose of this book is to describe these three
stages and the process of their gradual combination and
recomposition.

Talk about more than one writer of the book of Amos
almost invariably leads to a notion of an original prophet
surrounded by secondary additions. It is then nearly impossible to avoid the implication that the original words are more
true than those belonging to subsequent recomposition, no
matter what importance the latter might have. And so we end
up neglecting precisely the source of meaning we need to
discover in order to understand the flow of prophecy: not the
prophet or addition alone, but their interplay and synthesis.
Others may feel that the concept of many composers jeopardizes the authority of the book of Amos and therefore represents an unsatisfactory interpretive tool. I believe our task is
to work out the implications of this concept for our understanding and faith, not to shy away from it, ignore it, or
negate it.

I have three reasons. First, the concept is an historical fact.
The book of Amos was composed by more than one person.
Faith that ignores facts runs the risk of becoming faith that
doesn't matter.

Second, far from regretting that the book of Amos is the
end result of a process of recomposition, I am grateful. The
reason is simple: if it were not, we would not have it. Each
stage of recomposition represents an interpretation of
Amos's words, and thus an actualization of them, a reading
and understanding of them that makes them real and important in a new and different present. Without these successive actualizations, the words of Amos would soon have been

forgotten. These actualizations are earlier analogues of our own interpretation of Amos by which we make it meaningful to us. The life of the word in the community of faith depends on continuously reactualizing the word. To say the recomposers of the book of Amos may not meaningfully do so is to imply that we may not. To say that they may, and to take them seriously at it, allows us to see ourselves in direct continuity with the persons and communities of faith that read Amos so actively that they rewrote him as they read. Our Scriptures *came into being in the process of interpretation.*

Third, since in the course of recomposition neither Amos nor the subsequent composers got lost, the little book of Amos contains within it some fundamental tenets of faith locked together in all their tension and contradiction. We, too, strive to include among ourselves these basic tenets. To see how they are contained in the book of Amos can give us a glimpse of how we might include them. The greatest paradox of the process of recomposition is its greatest benefit: at the same time that it resolves theological tensions, it maintains them. That, after all, is the benefit of the Bible itself. Who would reject such a benefit?

In this book I'll be talking about Amos and additions to his words in a very limited sense. Whatever form the words of Amos took when they were first spoken and then written down, as soon as they were rewritten in any way differently, they changed and acquired new meaning. In fact, as soon as they were *written,* and thus translated into a new medium, their meaning changed. What other changes could produce new meanings? The most obvious change is in the words themselves. Others are slightly more subtle. Think of the ways by which the news media transmit quotes from newsmakers: adding words or phrases before or after the quote, rearranging parts, eliminating parts, or creating a different context. All these techniques play a role in the book of Amos. Recomposition is like the history-making process. Events are not history. History involves selection, retelling, organizing, and relating—steps that make history an art, something based on events but not the same as the events. The words of Amos are like events to which we no longer have direct, undistorted access. When I refer to the words of Amos, I mean the words reconstructed from later editions, but in their original context.

Thereafter these same words take on new contexts and change meaning in successive editions. I prefer to speak of editions rather than additions. The successive editions of the words of Amos were composed along with words from traditions no less prophetic than that of Amos. More importantly, the inclusion of these other words with Amos's words represents a claim for their authority equal to the claim for the authority of the words of Amos—a claim we are in a position to examine but not to deny.

There is an easy way to grasp this process of composition and recomposition and its implications for understanding the book of Amos. The following metaphor was suggested to me by a student early in my thinking about Amos. It is a bit algebraic but serves its purpose well. Suppose author A composed some separate short works (oracles, for example), which we can call 2, 4, and 6. Later editor B, to some extent making use of prophetic tradition (perhaps even some of other A material), composed a similar group—let's call them 3, 5, and 7—to express the concerns of his own person and time. Appropriating A's 2, 4, and 6, B preserved them (possibly modifying them slightly) by joining them to his own words, and composed a new work, 2b-3-4b-5-6b-7, in which 2b stands for A's 2 as preserved or modified by B, 3 for B's 3, and so forth. Then came editor C, who rewrote this work with the addition of an opening and closing, which we'll call 1 and 8. These parts were written for the purpose of introducing and concluding the work, or drawn from A's and B's or some other prophetic tradition and modified for that purpose. This new work gives a third slant to the words of A and another to the words of B. It can be schematized as 1-2bc-3c-4bc-5c-6bc-7c-8, in which 1 stands for C's 1, 2bc for B's 2b as preserved or modified by C, 3c for B's 3 as preserved or modified by C, and so forth.

Now who would you say is the author of part 2bc? Obviously all three are: A, B, and C. Just as obviously, however, it is C's version of 2bc that we have, not A's or B's. It is editor C and his work to which we have the most direct access, if only because his is the only complete work we have. In the case of author A, all we have of his work now is 2bc, 4bc, and 6bc. We can no longer be certain of the order and exact wording of any part except 1 and 8. The critic's task is to delineate as fully and accurately as possible the work of author A and editors B and C. The result will be not only an understanding of longer segments of prophecy—in this case, of the successive editions of the book of Amos—but also a fuller understanding of each oracle within them.

Such overlapping composition results in something like *Intelligent Life in the Universe,* by I. S. Shklovskii and Carl Sagan (San Francisco: Holden-Day, Inc., 1966). Shklovskii first wrote a short book in Russian on extraterrestrial life. When Sagan translated it into English, he doubled its length by interspersing his own contributions throughout and turned it into a college textbook on astronomy. Unlike the successive editors of the oracles of Amos, Sagan changed nothing in the original except the language. He even marked the sections containing Shklovskii's original so they could be distinguished from his own contributions. (A similar procedure used in Amos would have obviated this book!)

A parallel that may more closely resemble the end result of a prophetic book is the holiday phone call from the family. While you listen passively, Dad, Mom, and Sis, one after another and in rapid and mixed succession, grab the other end of the line and tell their own news, worries, and desires, some related and some not. You have no trouble telling which words come from which speaker by the sound of their voices. Now could you identify the speaker if you had only a transcript of such a call? You probably could. In the same way the voices of the editors of Amos become identifiable, after we get to know them.

This book is essentially an essay in redaction criticism. The view, however, that a prophetic book grows around a core tradition over a period of time in continuous interaction with changing historical circumstances owes a great deal to tradition criticism, or tradition history, an approach to Old Testament study of particular significance during the last half century. One of the most influential works in tradition criticism, Gerhard von Rad's *Old Testament Theology*, deals with the entire Old Testament from this perspective. The view I follow represents a considerable departure from von Rad in two respects. First, von Rad takes most of the book of Amos to be the words of Amos, most of the book of Hosea to be the words of Hosea, and so on. As already pointed out, scholars are now coming to understand that almost every prophetic book is instead a complex tapestry of strands from different tradition sources, perhaps more like the current picture of the composition of the Pentateuch than anything else. Second, for von Rad each individual prophet's work represents a step forward in the gradual development of prophecy through history. Each prophet had a new idea to contribute.

The view of this book, which today may be more widely held than von Rad's, is that the constituent strands of a prophetic book, or what I am calling its stages, do not represent discrete moments in a unilinear development of prophecy, but rather differing modes and concerns from a wide range of prophetic traditions. It seems that the whole range of what we now have as prophetic traditions existed in one form or another throughout the monarchic period. Distinctive versions of these traditions were edited into the different prophetic books at different stages. While building on the insights of fifty years of tradition criticism, I believe it is important to incorporate the refinements that have occurred since von Rad, particularly in the areas of literary and social history.

Some will recognize that, in terms of redaction criticism, my view of the growth of Amos is closer to that of H. W. Wolff and R. F. Melugin than to that of Klaus Koch, though not dependent on any of these.

In this book I will label the three successive stages of the recomposition of the book of Amos as A, B, and C. Stage A is the edition of Amos—it is doubtful that the first recorder of Amos's words in writing was Amos himself, but no one knows for sure. Stage B is the edition of someone I'll call the

Bethel editor for reasons that will become quickly apparent when we deal with this second edition in detail. Stage C is the work of someone I'll call the closing editor.

The A stage was composed roughly in the eighth century (before 722 B.C.), the B stage in the seventh century, between the time of Hezekiah and Josiah, or slightly later, and the C stage in the sixth century, near the end of the Babylonian exile or shortly thereafter. The A stage condemns and announces disaster, the B stage admonishes and offers a choice, and the C stage promises a restitution. I like to characterize the stages in terms of parenting: the A stage represents the parent's anger and hostility, destructive and unproductive. The B stage represents the parent's warning, which risks inviting the very behavior it rejects, and the C stage the parent's love, mercy, and trust, but also discrimination. The A stage views life as a task we have failed at, the B stage life as a task, and the C stage life as a gift. The stages differ considerably in their style, but style cannot be easily summarized, so I leave it for later, when I can give it the coverage it requires.

Of course, these descriptions are generalizations. At most they describe the emphases of the different stages. But they give some hint of what we will be looking at in this book. For the time being let them serve as guideposts to territories we will shortly be exploring in much more detail.

Before going on I want to stress two caveats regarding the scheme developed so far. The first is this: to reduce the composition of the book of Amos to a three-stage process is an oversimplification. I have already indicated my awareness of that. H. W. Wolff's recent commentary on Amos makes a similar analysis in terms of six stages. This book is not a commentary. It is an essay, not a reference work (hence no index). I intend to keep the analysis simple enough to be easily followed and genuinely useful for understanding Amos and, with adaptation, other prophetic books. I believe this is possible without misrepresenting the development of the book of Amos. When you have read the chapter on the second stage, you may even be able to analyze it further into more detailed stages, on the basis of your reading. (Another way I have oversimplified is to present the recomposition of Amos as though it took place primarily in isolation from the recomposition of many other documents, prophetic and otherwise. The opposite was true.)

The second caveat is even more important: the concerns stressed in each successive stage coexisted among prophets throughout the period of the formation of the book of Amos. For instance, prophets admonished and prophets promised restitution during the time of Amos, even though we are calling these B-stage and C-stage concerns in the book of Amos. What we are identifying in this analysis are the successive stages in which these concerns found literary expression in the editions of the words of Amos. This is a very specific matter. It is not my purpose to describe the history of prophetic faith in general. In fact, the analysis of stages of composition has to be done separately for each prophetic book. On occasion I will repeat this caveat because it is easy, in the context of the last century of critical study, to forget it.

I have two final comments. The first is about translation. The convention in books of this type is to quote the Bible from some widely used translation. This convention limits the contribution such books might have made to the understanding of Scripture. It is based on the idea, usually held unconsciously, that translation is objective and interpretation is subjective. Such an idea allows us to feel secure that we may understand a text on the basis of a translation, but it ignores at least two experiences had by many persons who have read the Bible for years in its original languages. The first is that, with anyone's translation, success is a matter of degree. A translation usually conveys only part of the meaning of the original and is often uncertain. T. S. Eliot said poetry is what gets lost in translation. In a less extreme way, the same is true of the Bible. The other experience is that, since translation represents an interpretation, it ought to do so intentionally. In this book I present an interpretation of a Hebrew text, not of an English translation. (I hasten to say you don't need Hebrew to read this book.) The translation, therefore, is my own and as much as possible reflects my understanding. Critical readers will want to compare my translation with others they regularly use. Sometimes these other translations may bring out even better than my own the point I am making. But they are not my starting point.

My other comment is about chapter and verse numbers. I have avoided them when possible without inconveniencing the reader. They came very late to the Biblical text. Even many of the earliest printed Bibles lack them. They perform for us the task of dividing the text into meaningful segments, a task that we all ought to be doing for ourselves. They imply that the text is minutely fragmented. They suggest that an identifying code can stand for the words themselves. We can do with less of them.

2
The Prophet Amos:
Stage A

The oracles of Amos announce the annihilation of the ruling elite in eighth-century Samaria. If you read all of these oracles at once in a group, you can see how much they have in common and how distinctive they are. I cite them here in the order they follow in the book of Amos, but remember this order was probably determined by the B editor and does not tell anything certain about the order in which Amos delivered them. If you follow along in a familiar translation, which I encourage, you'll notice differences. Some of these are based on a different understanding of the Hebrew. A few come from emendation or from the removal of phrases added by the B or C editors. One probable gloss appears in brackets, and one oracle is rearranged (an explanation follows in chapter 3).

THE ORACLES
    Thus says Yahweh:
    Because they sell the righteous for money
        And the needy for a pair of sandals
    Those which shuffle after the dust of the earth
        [on the head of the poor]
        And shunt aside the custom of the indigent
    The man and his father who go to the girl
        To profane my holy name
    Who stretch out on garments taken in pledge
        And drink the wine of those they mulct
    I am about to . . . beneath them as a cart . . . that is
        loaded with sheaves (the word left untranslated is
        obscure).

Flight will vanish from the swift
  The strong will not regain his strength
  The warrior will not rescue his life
The bowman will not stand fast
  The swift of foot will not escape
The strongest-willed among the warriors will flee naked
  on that day—oracle of Yahweh.

* * *

Proclaim upon the strongholds in Ashdod
  And upon the strongholds in the land of Egypt
Say, "Gather upon the mount of Samaria
  And view the great rout within it.
  Those who have suffered extortion in her midst
They do not know right action—oracle of Yahweh—
  Who treasure up violence and plunder in their strong-
    holds."
Therefore, thus says the lord Yahweh
The foe! The land is surrounded!
  He will bring down from you your strength
  Your strongholds will be plundered.

* * *

Thus says Yahweh: as a shepherd recovers two chops or
a piece of ear from the mouth of a lion, so the Israelites
who dwell comfortably in Samaria will be recovered—
with a piece of a couch leg and a fancy chip from the bed.

* * *

Hear this word, O cows of Bashan in the mount of
  Samaria
  Who extort from the poor
  Who crunch the needy
  Who say to their lords
  "Bring, that we may drink!"
The lord Yahweh has sworn by his holiness: days are on
  their way—against you.
You will be carried away in baskets
  Every last one of you in fish pots
Through the breaches you will go out, one after another
  To be thrown out . . . (end obscure).

* * *

Hear this word I raise over you in lamentation

The virgin Israel has fallen down—
  no more to rise
She is left abandoned on the ground—
  no one to raise her.

* * *

Because they levy excessive rents upon the poor
  And take exactions in wheat from them
Who attack the righteous, who take a bribe
  And so shunt aside the needy in the gate
Therefore the fine stone houses you have built—
  you shall not dwell in them
The delightful vineyards you have planted—
  you shall not drink their wine.

* * *

Therefore thus says Yahweh
In all the squares there shall be wailing
  And in all the streets they shall say, "Ho! Ho!"
And they shall invite the peasant to mourning
  And to wailing those who know how to lament
In all the vineyards there shall be wailing
  For I will pass through your midst.
Yahweh has spoken.

* * *

Woe! to those who desire the day of Yahweh
  What is the day of Yahweh to you
  It is darkness, and not light
As when a man flees from a lion and a bear meets him,
and he enters his house and leans his hand against the
wall and a snake bites him
Darkness is the day of Yahweh, and not light
  Gloom it is, with no brightness.

* * *

Woe! to those at ease in . . . (a C-stage word may have
  displaced the original)
  To those who feel secure on the mount of Samaria
The designated men of the prime of the nations
  To whom the house of Israel come
Pass by Kullani* and see.

* Instead of Kalneh; see below, page 118.

13

From there go to Hamath the great
Then go down to Gath of the Philistines.
Are you better than these kingdoms?
Is your territory greater than their territory?
You who put off the evil day
Who bring near the life of violence
Who lie upon couches decorated with inlaid ivory work
Prostrate upon their divans
Eating lambs from the flock
Calves from the midst of the stall
Singing to the lead of the harp,
Improvising for themselves on instruments of song
Who drink from ample wine bowls
And anoint with the prime of oils
But are not laid up for the breaking of Joseph
Therefore they shall go into exile at the head of the exiles
And the *marzech*-feast of the prostrate will pass away.

* * *

The lord Yahweh has sworn by himself: Yahweh is
about to give the command
He will smite the large house into fragments
And the small house into splinters.

* * *

Hear this, you who shuffle after the needy
To destroy the oppressed of the land
Saying, "When will the New Moon feast pass, that we
may sell grain
And the Sabbath feast, that we may offer wheat for
sale?
To use too small a dry measure
To use too heavy a counterweight
To crook the fraudulent balance
To buy the poor for money
And the needy for a pair of sandals
That we may sell the refuse of the wheat?"
Yahweh has sworn by the glory of Jacob, "I shall never
forget their deeds."
On that day—oracle of the lord Yahweh—
I will make the sun set at noon
And I will darken the earth in broad daylight
I will turn your pilgrimage feasts into mourning
And all your songs into lamentation

I will bring sackcloth upon all loins
    And baldness (of mourning) upon every head
I will make her like mourning for an only son
    And her very last one like the day a last child dies.

* * *

Strike the topstone so the thresholds quake
    And slash away at the heads of all of them
    Every last one of them I will slay by the sword
Not one of them shall flee
    Not one of them shall escape.
If they grovel into Sheol
    From there my hand shall take them
If they go up to the sky
    From there I will bring them down
If they hide on the top of Carmel
    From there I will search out and take them
If they hide from my sight on the bottom of the ocean
    From there I will command the snake, and it shall bite
        them
If they go into captivity with their enemies behind
    From there I will command the sword, and it shall slay
        them.

Other passages in the book of Amos may contain words, phrases, and even lines that go back to Amos himself. These would help explain the distinctiveness of the whole book of Amos as compared with other prophetic books. In this group I have included only the oracles of Amos that are for the most part intact. Other passages, even when they contain words going back to Amos, lack the distinctiveness of Amos and display their own distinctiveness to such a degree that they are better dealt with in terms of later stages of the book.

DISTINCTIVE FEATURES OF AMOS A

It was possible to make such a selection of the oracles of Amos only after a lengthy study of the book, with a good deal of necessarily circular reasoning. But now that we can read them this way in a group, the distinctive features they have in common become readily apparent. There are nine of them. Once you become familiar with those of the later stages as well, the distinctive features of the A-stage oracles will grab you by the collar.

1. These oracles are addressed to a *specific* class of persons in a *specific* place and time. Contrast "Woe to those who feel secure on the mount of Samaria" with "Seek good and not evil." The first one is specific about person, place, and—by implication—time, whereas the other could be addressed to almost anyone, in any place, at any time (it belongs to the B stage). The addressees of the A stage are the secure, the strong, the well-to-do, the well-housed and well-fed, the authorities, the holders of power and privilege—in short, the ruling elite of Israel's agrarian society. (The ruling elite are the few who rule. The word elite has a pejorative sound. I want to use it in its neutral sense of the select few and leave the moral characterization of the people it denotes—a complex issue for the historian—to fuller description and discussion.) These elite live in towns throughout the northern kingdom of Israel, but they concentrate in Samaria, the capital and primary center of urban power. They live prior to the fall of Samaria in 722 B.C. to the Assyrians.

2. These oracles all contribute to a *single basic message*. The powerful have oppressed the powerless; the ruling elite, the poor. In the midst of this oppression, in fact on the very foundation of it, the powerful enjoy a luxury whose most offensive manifestation is an extravagant festivity. God rejects this state of affairs and will reverse it. In a typical measure-for-measure response of justice, God will answer the violence done to the powerless by the elite with his own violence against the elite. He will wage war against them, killing many and leading others into exile, where they too will be killed. God will answer their festive revelry by turning it, through war, into lamentation and wailing. For oppression, war. For revelry, wailing. These four terms sum up the whole basic message of the prophet Amos.

3. These oracles share a set of *stylistic features* that set them off from oracles belonging to the later stages. Notice how certain phrases get repeated, like the destruction of "every last one," or how certain ideas keep recurring, like the five references to the vine and wine, usually near breaks in the

oracle when indictment turns to judgment. We can say that these phrases and ideas are typical of Amos.

These oracles are composed in *poetry*, a nearly invariable feature of preexilic prophecy and a feature whose significance can hardly be overstressed. The poetry of the A stage stands out by its (a) consistent parallelism, (b) rough equivalency of line length, which usually survives recomposition, (c) vivid use of language, and (d) concrete visual imagery. The few original nonpoetic lines that occur in the oracles of Amos usually come at junctures and thus show their own distinctiveness.

The distinctiveness of the poetry of these oracles is more evident in Hebrew than in most English translations. Because it is known that prophecy is supposed to be poetry, the edition of the Hebrew Bible that most scholars use arranges more of the book of Amos on the page as poetry than actually is poetry, at least in its more consistent preexilic form. The translators of Amos have simply followed suit. Thus most translations give a misleading impression of the quantity of poetry, hence blurring this essential means of identifying the oracles of Amos. Oracles belonging to later stages of the book also contain some poetry, but far less frequently, more sporadically, and with different characteristics.

4. These oracles were delivered *orally*. (It is important to distinguish between oral delivery and oral composition; whether they were orally composed is impossible to say.) The oracles' forms copy oral forms. The stories about the prophets indicate they usually spoke outdoors. Perhaps they employed an attention-getting tone, something like the piercing twang called "hard singing" often heard in cultures where bel canto and the bullhorn are less prevalent than in ours. Amos's penchant for dramatic rhetoric—climax, direct quotes, rhetorical questions—may also point to his oral delivery.

5. These oracles speak *directly*. Their message of condemnation is straightforward, unqualified, and categorical. They do not deal in ironic reversals for a positive outcome as the later stages do. They use wordplay and irony to compound their direct meaning rather than to qualify or undermine it.

For instance, the line "Those which shuffle after the dust of the earth" refers to both elite and sandals, and to both the poor and dirt, the latter two being the same in the view of the elite. The unoriginal gloss plainly dissolves the irony. Similarly, "in all the streets they shall say, 'Ho! Ho!' " indicates there is a banquet for everyone. But the wail of invitation (*ho* or *hoy*) merges with the wail of woe (*hoy*): look at Isa. 55:1 in Hebrew, if you can, to see this merging (compare Zech. 2:6–7 [Eng.], 2:10–11 [Heb.]). Thus, "they invite the peasant to mourning." The feast will be their oppressors! Reread that oracle so you can see how many words in it contribute to this ironic jerk. The B editor places two woe oracles immediately following, as though Ho! meant only Woe! His unoriginal organization dissolves the A-stage irony.

6. These oracles employ a *limited repertoire of short forms*: judgment, oath, announcement of war, and dirge. These forms blend with one another in various effective ways. Nearly all the full lines preserved from Amos seem to be part of some oracle extant in its entirety. There are few if any separate lines running loose, as it were. One less than certain case is Yahweh's command to smite the houses into fragments and splinters. Although it is an announcement of war, it is uncharacteristically short and may not be complete. It may be part of the sentence of the preceding oracle. The line about rescuing couch and bed chips is in a class by itself, though its message and vocabulary leave no doubt it goes back to Amos.

7. The *meaning* of one oracle is *not dependent on* its *juxtaposition* with the others, or even on being read in any way in combination with the others. In other words, the meaning of these oracles is self-contained. Despite the independence of the oracles, however, as well as the unlikelihood that their present order goes back to Amos, they do have some coherence in their present arrangement. You may find it interesting to read through the oracles again from beginning to end to look for signs of their overall coherence. Once you start noticing them, their number will surprise you. I have wondered whether this might be an indication that the B editor

used some prior collection of oracles. There is no way to know. The main point to keep in mind is that each oracle by itself announces the same basic message; none requires for its understanding a particular place in a larger literary whole or rigid train of thought.

8. These oracles announce an *inevitable catastrophe*. They leave no way to squirm out of it. Their forms insist on it. Yahweh has passed judgment and imposed the sentence: war, exile, and death. Yahweh has published his war orders: *de guello*, no quarter. He has taken a solemn oath to carry them out. Amos chants a dirge. "Woe to those at ease in Samaria": you are as good as dead. Your obituary has just come out. The assertion of ineluctability is especially noticeable where the indictment is expressed in a dirge. There may be no law against extravagant revelry per se, and thus a simple judgment may not convincingly apply, but you will go into exile for it nevertheless. The inevitability of the oracles of Amos is implied by their very preservation. They are preserved because they were validated by the destruction, exile, and death they announce. God's sentence of death can be interpreted by the events that burst in after it.

9. These oracles are *fulfillable,* and they were *fulfilled* in 722 B.C. They could be fulfilled again. The composer of the C stage certainly understood them to have been fulfilled again, in 587 B.C., when the ruling elite of Judah were taken into exile to Babylon. But their specificity is such that they were first fulfilled when Assyria sacked Samaria and removed the Israelite ruling elite into exile, there to vanish.

AMOS AND HIS TIME

What do these oracles tell us about Amos? Some of our ideas about Amos, or what we currently read about him, depend on passages that do not share these features and so ought not to be included in this stage. Oracles from the later stages of composition may contain information useful for talking historically about Amos and other eighth-century prophets, but it is necessary to examine the oracles of this first stage of composition, which definitely go back to Amos, to see what can be found out on the basis of them alone. An example of how this procedure makes a difference is the dating of Amos.

When did Amos prophesy? The book of Amos itself gives an answer to that question: "in the days of Uzziah king of Judah and in the days of Jeroboam son of Joash, king of Israel, two years before the quaking." It goes on to mention Jeroboam twice more in the story of Amos's visit to Bethel. A new chronology of the kings of Israel and Judah prepared recently and distributed privately by F. M. Cross assigns Uzziah's rule to about 781–747 and Jeroboam II's rule to about 781–745. Introductory treatments of Amos comment on the relative peace and prosperity in northern Israel during this period. Assyria, the main threat to peace on the horizon, was harassed by the expanding kingdom of Urartu far to the northeast, out of the Syro-Palestinian arena altogether. During the lull in activity on its eastern front, Damascus, Israel's hostile neighbor during much of the preceding two centuries, engaged in a lengthy military struggle with Hamath and other Aramean states to its north. In the midst of this letup in international pressure, Jeroboam presided over a resurgence of Israelite hegemony, to judge from 2 Kings 14:25–28. (This passage presents problems of interpretation deserving treatment in their own right before it can be used as direct historical information.) According to many biblical archaeologists, the quality of architecture and pottery in Israel, the occurrence of ivory inlay, and the evidence of flourishing local crafts all indicate that in the first half of the eighth century Israel enjoyed a marked increase in prosperity.

This picture of the time of Amos is based entirely on the naming of Jeroboam II. But the oracles of Amos that can be assigned to the A stage do not name Jeroboam II, and in other ways they cast doubt on the view that Amos prophesied during his reign. According to these oracles, Amos announced an impending deportation of the ruling elite. Deportation did not become a significant article of Assyrian imperialistic policy until the reign of Tiglath-pileser III (745–727), who acceded to the Assyrian throne the year Jeroboam died and did not carry out his policy of deportation in the west until seven years later.

The places named in the A-stage oracles point to the time of Tiglath-pileser III. To begin with, Assyria is *not* mentioned. (Most scholars regard the Greek reading of Assyria for Ashdod in 3:9 that appears in many translations as not original.) That means the Assyrian threat is so imminent that it is taken for granted. Such a threat fits the period of Assyrian strength under Tiglath-pileser III better than the preceding period of Assyrian distraction. In one oracle, Amos recalls Kullani, Hamath, and Gath as though they had been recently overpowered by the Assyrians. Both Kullani and Hamath, in the vicinity of each other to the north of Israel, were conquered by the Assyrians during Tiglath-pileser's first major campaign to the west, in 738. Although not mentioned in the Assyrian account thereof, Gath may have been conquered during Tiglath-pileser's second major campaign to the west in 734, when he controlled a large part of Philistine territory. Other possibilities are later, not earlier. Ashdod seems to enjoy independence in Amos's time. Although it was under tribute to Judah at least once in the first half of the century, by the time of Sargon II (722–705), and probably before, it had regained its autonomy, until it was taken by the Assyrians in 711.

Because of gaps in our knowledge of Assyrian campaigns to the west during the entire period in question, and because cities alternately came under Assyrian control and regained their freedom with bewildering frequency, we cannot expect the few facts available to provide a definitive picture of the events to which the oracles of Amos refer. The historical evaluation, furthermore, of the place names mentioned in the oracles of the A stage must take into consideration the rhetorical circumstances that may have led to the choice of these names from presumably many possibilities. For example, the names Ashdod and Egypt represent wordplays on "plunder" and "foe," respectively. Gath means "winepress" and thus may be chosen for naming in order to reinforce whatever message is being conveyed by the emphasis on wine at various breaking points in the collected oracles. Kullani and Hamath, which together fell in 738, provide the least ambiguous historical references. All in all, indications are that Amos prophesied not during the reign of Jeroboam II but rather during that of his successors, the contemporaries of Tiglath-pileser III.

Why then is Jeroboam II named in the book of Amos? One answer could be that Amos prophesied both during the reign of Jeroboam II and after it. But nothing in the A-stage oracles points directly to the reign of Jeroboam II. The references to Jeroboam belong to the B stage of composition. This is evident immediately from the naming of Uzziah, the king of Judah, before Jeroboam, the king of Israel, in the heading of the book. (Other reasons will be given in chapter 3.) The heading is a Judean, seventh-century statement. We could ask whether by then people had forgotten when Amos prophesied. But there is a more pertinent question: what function does the naming of Jeroboam serve? This question could only be addressed adequately after we become acquainted with the B stage. For now, recall that the B editor is particularly concerned with Bethel, and that the name of the founder of the cult at Bethel according to deuteronomistic tradition was Jeroboam—Jeroboam I, the first king of the northern kingdom of Israel. Amos, the B-stage story tells us, confronted (through his priest) the *namesake* of the founder of the cult of Bethel. Even from this brief discussion, it is clear that the name Jeroboam contributes to an important B-stage concern.

According to the B-stage story, furthermore, Amos announces that Jeroboam will die by the sword. There is no indication in 2 Kings 14:29 that Jeroboam II died other than a peaceful death. Amos's prediction does not apply to Jeroboam, but it could apply to four of the five kings who followed him on the throne of Israel, the four kings murdered during the span of fourteen years, 745–732. If Amos did prophesy against kings (notice 7:9 "the house, or descendants, of Jeroboam"), the phrase "die by the sword" may be left from such prophecies. In that case it would corroborate other indications that Amos prophesied during the reign of Tiglath-pileser III.

If Amos prophesied after Jeroboam II and closer to the events he predicts, he must be looked at from a perspective different from the customary one in four ways. Not only does he not prophesy to Jeroboam, but he doesn't prophesy to *any* specific king. In the first place, then, Amos addresses a *class*, the ruling elite in Samaria, rather than individuals. If a king is included in his indictment, it is because the king is the pinnacle of that class. Thus to hear the oracles of Amos on their own terms is to shift attention from the individuality of the reigning king to the conspiracy of king and ruling class.

Second, not only does the individuality of the king lose significance, but the individuality of the prophet loses it, too. The awareness that Amos prophesied closer to 722 than previously thought brings into question the picture of one or two great individual prophets hovering ominously over northern Israel for decades, in person and memory, as lone spokesmen for justice. If you put Amos's oracles next to the clearly genuine oracles of Hosea, Micah, or Isaiah, you won't find significant differences in their descriptions of injustice. Although he was a unique individual, as a prophet Amos was one of a type. Even his name, which means "burden" or "delivery" and therefore probably "oracle," like similar words in Hebrew and Phoenician, suggests typicality rather than individuality. Amos was singled out from the many unknown prophets who shared his vision of God's justice because he prophesied so close to the event. He was the one whom people remembered best.

The identity of the prophet and the source of his authority (the two are always yoked) carry greater weight in the B stage than in the A stage. That the B editor has to "borrow" Amos's authority already indicates his concern for it. His exhortations provoke the question of authority with greater importunity than Amos's descriptions. If to Amos one responds, "You don't say," to the B stage one responds, "Who says?" The message of B-stage tradition needs a boost of authority. It claims that Bethel is bad and Jerusalem, good. That is not so self-evident as Amos's assertion that injustice is bad. So the B stage needs to establish explicitly the authority by which it makes such a claim. When eventually Bethel's destruction itself contributes to the authority of the B-stage document, Amos's identity and authority are still essential for backing the B stage's problematic blend of justice and power.

A third way this modified perspective on Amos makes a difference grows out of the first two. It has to do with our notion of history. It goes without saying that prophecy needs to be interpreted in its historical context. For a long time this has tended to mean political context, the interactions of nations and influential persons. Thus the historical period of Amos is sketched chiefly in terms of the movements of nations and the activities of their rulers. I wonder whether we have too hastily latched on to the names of Jeroboam and Amos to satisfy this need for a history that is political and personal. Such history has its importance, but it ought to be seen as a part of a wider history in which other factors are given more attention than they have had until now. When the significance of these individuals as individuals is reduced, it is easier to make greater use of generic social categories in understanding Amos and his time.

This brings me to my fourth point. The social history of eighth-century Israel makes clear from still another perspective that the conditions indicated by the oracles of Amos are more likely to exist not in the time of peace during the reign of Jeroboam II, but in the time of international distress and domestic instability during the reigns of his successors.

AMOS'S SOCIETY

Monarchic Israel represents an advanced agrarian society. In such a society agriculture is the primary means of subsistence, the metal-tipped plow is the basis of agriculture, and tools and weapons are made out of iron. Sociologists have found that societies defined by these criteria—once the kind of society most human beings lived in—share many other characteristics that grow out of these basic ones. The most important characteristic of an advanced agrarian society is the extreme social cleavage between its two main classes, the ruling elite and peasantry.

Ruling Elite. The ruling elite are the governing class. Comprising from 1 to 3 percent of the population, they typically own 50 to 70 percent or more of the land. On the basis of these disproportionate land holdings, they control by far the greater amount of power and wealth in the society, and from their positions of power exercise domain over the peasantry. Although they own most of the land, the large majority live in cities, especially the capital. Many poor dwell in the city and some of the elite in rural towns, but because of their power and privilege the elite seldom come into meaningful social contact with the peasantry. They take virtually no role at all in the work on the land.

The ruling elite possess a body of cultural information so different from that of the peasantry that the gap between the two classes produces two distinct subcultures within the same society. Members of the elite subculture have been known to fail to recognize the peasant or urban poor as fellow human beings. According to Gerhard and Jean Lenski, a peasant's family was described as his "brood" in legal documents drawn up by the ruling elite in the Middle Ages, and estate records in Europe, Asia, and America often listed the peasants with the livestock. In India, a peasant is called a *ryot,* from an Arabic word meaning a member of the "herd." In Israel, the blessing God bestowed on the righteous consists of material prosperity. It therefore seems sensible to the elite to regard themselves as the righteous. Their wealth proves it! They take for granted that the poor's poverty reflects some lack of righteousness. This is to define one's status in God's sight exclusively in terms of the present, which the prophetic perspective contradicts. Since justice is hard to achieve, doubtless the paucity of the elite confirms their sense of righteousness. Righteousness is for the few, they believe. From the stance of power, self-deception is hard to correct.

The link between power and wealth in advanced agrarian societies and the concentration of power and wealth in the hands of the few result in what can be called a command, as opposed to demand, economy. The forces of supply and demand are much less important than the arbitrary, self-serving decisions of the elite. This is why Amos addresses the ruling elite as he does, on the premise that through their actions they have a direct effect on the economy.

Peasantry. The peasantry are the cultivators of the land. They make up from 60 to 80 percent or more of a typical agrarian society. After they have drawn from what they produce on the land whatever they need for subsistence, replacement (what they need to continue farming), and ceremony, they transfer the surplus, as it is euphemistically called, to the ruling elite. The elite use these peasant surpluses to support themselves both directly and through distribution to aides, merchants, craftsmen, and other groups who do not farm but contribute to the elite's standard of living.

Almost universally the peasant lives on the margin of subsistence. The surplus flows steadily from countryside to city in payment of rents, taxes, tribute, tithes, interest on debts, fines, and "gifts" to the ruling elite. The rents are common and numerous, given the percentage of land owned by the ruling elite.

The elite often own not only the land but also the peasants, in varying degrees of serfdom and slavery. Even when peasants own the land they work, they often find it difficult to maintain their independence or to survive. There is too little margin for the difficulties that the single cultivator faces in the course of a few years of harvests. If there is a crop failure, for example, the peasant may be forced to borrow money, often at excessively high interest rates. The chances are that such a peasant may never again get out of debt.

The plight of the peasant in the unjust social order addressed by Amos in eighth-century Israel was the direct result of two main factors: (1) the shift from the predominance of patrimonial domain to prebendal domain, and (2) the role of the ruling elite in encouraging, manipulating, and profiting from this shift.

The Shift in Domain. Domain involves both who has ultimate ownership or control over the land and how that control is exercised. There are two main kinds of domain. *Patrimonial* domain is exercised by persons who inherit ownership or control as members of kinship groups. In Israel ownership usually passed from father to son. Whatever its origin, the primary understanding of domain in Israel is patrimonial. Families or clans held domain over estates granted to them by Yahweh, to whom the land ultimately belonged, and in the long run this domain was inalienable. Clan lands were called "grants" (*nachlah,* usually translated "inheritance") because they were granted by Yahweh and held by patrimonial domain. At the village level, these were periodically redistributed among the local clans for the sake of equity. Thus we can describe this kind of domain in Israel as redistributional clan egalitarianism.

Prebendal domain is exercised by officials of a state by virtue of grants from a sovereign who holds ultimate ownership of the land. The officials therefore control not the land, which is owned by the sovereign, but the income from the land. These grants of income are known as prebends, and the officials who hold them as prebendal lords (Hebrew *sar,* usually translated "prince," can often mean prebendal lord). This form of domain is characteristic of states whose political organization is able to curtail heritable claims to land and rent (patrimonial domain) in favor of the eminent domain of a sovereign. The permanence of prebendal domain might be determined by custom, the will of the sovereign, and the political stability of the times. In Israel, the king distributed domain over lands he did not require for his own immediate use to servants (high officials), retainers, and other courtiers in return for political, bureaucratic, and military services useful to the king in his exercise of power. The king could, of course, retain a share of the prebendal income he granted to another. (The king could also grant a form of patrimonial domain over lands in his control; because in practice this form of domain was so easily revocable, however, in this book I have simplified the picture by considering all royal grants as essentially prebendal.)

The tendency was for the prevailing form of domain in Israel to shift from patrimonial to prebendal during the monarchic period, ca. 1000–600 B.C. An increasing number of historians of early Israel believe that the patrimonial domain characteristic of early Israel came into being as the result of peasant rebellion and land reform some two centuries prior to the first Israelite kings. In early Israel, patrimonial domain was instituted not in its usual sense, as a means whereby the elite class could continue to draw off the wealth of the peasantry, but in a more revolutionary sense, as a means whereby the peasantry themselves gained control over all their resources, including the surpluses that used to flow into the hands of their overlords. Thus the peasants of early Israel claimed that Yahweh was lord of the land and as such held eminent domain over the land in direct opposition to the claims of a mundane ruling elite.

Patrimonial, redistributional domain applied only to the lands in Israel's possession prior to the monarchy. These lands tended to be concentrated in the central hill country of Palestine (though not all of it was included) and to exclude the plains, wide valleys, and coastal hills where the urban ruling class ("Canaanites") continued to exercise effective military and therefore economic power. These flatter lands were in large part added to Israelite holdings by Israel's first kings, especially David and Solomon, through conquest and purchase. A typical instance of such acquisitions from some fifty years into the existence of the northern kingdom is Omri's purchase of the land on which Samaria was to be built (1 Kings 16:24). These newer lands were held mostly by the king through eminent domain and assigned personally to prebendal lords, rather than entered into the redistributional system of premonarchic patrimonial lands. At first, we may surmise, prebendal domain exercised over royal holdings developed alongside patrimonial domain exercised over premonarchic holdings. But, with power on its side, prebendal domain inevitably was extended to more and more areas formerly held by patrimonial domain. Small holdings held by grant from Yahweh were swallowed up by more extensive prebendal estates (compare 1 Kings 21), whose ultimate lord was to all intents and purposes not Yahweh but the king with other members of the ruling elite. This process is called latifundialization. As happens so often, the gains of land reform were lost, and by the time of Amos the peasantry were essentially no better off than they were before Israel ever came into existence.

The Role of the Elite. This shift in the form of domain in ancient Israel did not by itself give rise to the injustices described by Amos. "Although the *form of domain* as such is relevant to the way a peasant ecosystem is organized, providing the pattern for social relations, it is *the way the pattern is utilized by the power-holders which is decisive in shaping the profile of the total system*" (E. R. Wolf, p. 56, italics in original). The way the ruling elite of Israel exercised prebendal domain has been called rent capitalism. The peasant occupiers of the prebendal estates had not only to pay tribute for the use of the land, but also rent for the various means, or factors, of production, like water, seed, work animals, tools, human labor for assistance, and potentially many others. Under rent capitalism, the rents attached to such factors of production can be accumulated by a single lord, but they can also be sold to other lords. As the process of production is split into an ever greater number of production factors, each must be rented separately, usually for an equal number of uniformly valued parts of the total rent paid out for production. In other words, the more segmented factors required to produce a crop, the more it is going to cost to produce it. And the more lords the peasant may rent from, the more separate factors he is likely to have to rent.

> The nadir of this system is attained . . . when the sharecropping farmer does not touch more than a meager share of the work of his hands. But it is even possible to split up farm work itself (as in plowing, harvesting, sometimes care of trees, and so forth) and to pay for it with appropriate shares of the product. The concept of the operating unit begins to dissolve into a series of individual tasks, and corresponding claims on income. Such a process of splitting into several tasks to which

independent monetary values are assigned brings the peasant into debt for each of the various factors of production which he requires to make a crop. He may have to pay to get water, and if he does not have the money, he may have to borrow it and pay interest on it; or he may borrow money and pay interest to get tools or borrow work animals and pay a charge for their use.

Such a system quickly leads to attempts to turn the various titles of income into debt titles. Interest rates of 100 or 200 percent are not uncommon. The reasons for such high interest rates are several, partly economic, partly political. One economic factor is a product of high population density and relative scarcity of land, especially in zones of permanent farming with hydraulic agriculture: The demand for land drives up its price, and hence both the rents charged for its use and the rates of interest on loans incurred in the course of such use. Another economic factor is that the poverty of the population itself compels cultivators to use the income derived from production to feed themselves. Poverty implies that subsistence takes priority over investment, and renders many cultivators unable "to make ends meet." Hence they must seek to get money through loans, and often must use such money to cover their subsistence. The moneylender, however, does not get his benefits from the consumption of his creditors, but from their production. Both the aggregate demand of many cultivators for loans and the desire of the moneylender to maximize his returns from their production tend to drive up interest rates. Lending to such a population with only a minimal capacity for repayment, moreover, freezes capital; that is, the moneylender cannot always or easily recover his money whenever he needs it. This situation again acts to drive up interest rates.

But there are also political reasons for this phenomenon. Where there is political instability, there is also a steady turnover in those who hold claims to land and money. Landlords and moneylenders must thus attempt to gain as much from their claims during their lifetime or their time in office as they can. . . . An additional factor may be the existence of a class of landlords and moneylenders whose real interests lie in living in urban areas and in assuming political office, and who see the exploitation of the countryside as a quick way of accumulating wealth to use in their political and social ascendency (Wolf, pp. 55–56).

The peasant's plight was exacerbated by the Assyrian threat. The ruling elite regularly responded to international pressures by leaning on their sole source of livelihood. Whether to gain alliance with neighboring states against Assyria, to raise tribute to pay directly to Assyria, or to buy or make armaments for wars against Assyria, the result was the same: increased efforts to draw off ever larger portions of peasant production. Gottwald states the situation well:

> Early statist Israel capitalized on a period when no great empires imposed their wills on the ancient Near East. From the mid-ninth century, however, Assyria . . . intruded on the autonomy of Syro-Palestinian states in programs of economic and political domination intended to maximize the production, circulation, and concentration of international wealth to the advantage of the imperial metropolis [in Assyria].
>
> This intervention in Israel and Judah coincided with protracted internal social strife. To strengthen their positions vis-à-vis the threatening foreign powers, the Israelite states centralized and deployed their limited wealth—necessarily extracted from the peasants' precarious "surpluses"—for armaments and a favorable balance of trade. Monarchic war against foreign states was simultaneously . . . war against the mass of Israelite peasants. Land, the primary mode of production for the vast majority of Israelites, became subject to excessive taxation and to predatory merchant capital offered at exorbitant interest rates and issuing in debt slavery for growing numbers of impoverished Israelites (Gottwald, "Social and Economic Development," p. 466).

Under rent capitalism, the ruling elite could gain control of a large percentage of peasant production even without exercising prebendal domain over their lands. It is clear, however, that the elite used rent capitalism as a device to turn patrimonial lands into prebendal lands. A peasant's domain over his patrimony could not long withstand the economic strain of renting the multiplied factors of production. By the eighth century, once peasants had relinquished domain over their patrimony, nothing stood between them and eventual debt slavery. Many were forced into the landless labor pool and placed even more at the mercy of the elite.

In the time of Amos, a tiny ruling class residing in Samaria, driven by their need for power and wealth, impose an oppressive fragmentation of rentals on the Israelite peasantry, turning titles of income into titles of debt, including debt slavery. Their aim is to maximize the benefits from and the extent of their prebendal domain over peasant lands. Frequent and costly shifts in international alliances, along with severe domestic instability, force them to exercise power in an excessively harsh manner.

AMOS'S ANNOUNCEMENT

To this ruling class Amos announces: God will answer your war against the peasantry with war against you, and turn your festivity into lamentation. With a clearer picture of the societal conditions prevailing in the time of Amos, the terms of his announcement take on a new concreteness.

Oppression. Amos focuses on three aspects of the ruling class's "war" on the peasantry. The first is the oppressive way the ruling class exercise domain, and their gains and the peasant's losses therefrom. They "sell the righteous for money, the needy for a pair of sandals . . . ; stretch out on garments taken in pledge [legally these were not to be kept overnight], and drink the wine of those they mulct . . . ; treasure up violence [the fruits of extortion] and plunder . . . ; extort from the poor, crunch the needy . . . ; levy excessive rents upon the poor, and take exactions of wheat from them." The indictments that are translated in terms which seem abstract can be visualized on the basis of the societal picture drawn above. For example, "mulct" means to seize patrimonial lands for prebendal estates through the oppressive use of interest and fines. There's nothing abstract about that.

The second aspect is the venality of the ruling class. They pervert the "custom" of the peasantry, the common law of relief, remission, and just standards that the peasantry appeal to in grievance procedures against their overlords. The peasants haven't got a chance: overlord and judge belong to the same class, or at least the judge is decisively influenced from above. They "shuffle upon the dust of the earth, and shunt the custom of the indigent . . . ; attack the righteous and take a bribe, and so shunt the needy in the gate [where the elders of the ruling class sit to judge cases]."

The third aspect is the ruling class's promotion of a corrupt market and their manipulation of the economy. The produce obtained by duress from the peasantry comes back to them only after circulating through an urban market that artificially inflates its value. When the peasantry must resort to such a marketplace for their sustenance, their lives hang in the balance. The elite "use too small a dry measure, too heavy a counterweight, and crook the fraudulent balance."

The oracles of Amos reflect the exposure of a much larger segment of the agrarian economy to market forces, with their command basis, than serves the peasant's interests. The peasant engages in independent subsistence farming. Each family tends to grow a little of everything, consuming most of what they produce and producing most of what they consume. Archaeological evidence shows that during the first few centuries of occupation in the hill country mixed farming was widely practiced even there, despite the land's being better suited for the intensive cultivation of the vine. The peasants grow more grains than vines for good reasons: (1) wheat and barley make up a better diet than grapes, and (2) as long as the redistributional system operates and the land is realloted every seven years, the individual peasant is reluctant to risk losing in redistribution the investment in labor required to cultivate perennials like vines (as opposed to annuals like cereal crops).

What happens, however, as the hill country gradually comes under the prebendal domain of the ruling elite? They already control vast grain fields in the plains and valleys, lands that from the beginning were almost exclusively under prebendal domain. Naturally they desire to maximize their profit from their hill country acquisitions, best suited for vines. They do not have to worry about losing their investment in perennials after seven years. Although transport of the time does not allow major trade in most commodities, wine and oil are sufficiently compact and durable for the Samarian elite, in league with Phoenician merchants, to carry on a lucrative commerce dependent on the grape and olive, a commerce of no benefit to the peasantry. So these new land owners convert their hill country properties from mixed crops to vineyards and olive orchards. This changeover diminishes the quantity of grain directly available to the peasantry to a fraction of what they need, and they wind up in the marketplace bargaining at a grave disadvantage for grain they ought to have been allowed to grow for themselves. This is the calamity that incites Amos to condemn the elite for planting "pleasant vineyards" and to make vine and wine the cornerstone of his indictment.

Such exploitation continues to this day. The following was reported in *The Christian Science Monitor* on July 12, 1979:

> A year ago Amadeo Isabello was the proud member of a prosperous, self-sufficient Filipino farming village that grew rice, corn, avocados, and fruit trees.
>
> Today he is a slum dweller on the fringes of Manila, scrounging just to keep something—anything—on the dinner table for his nine-member family.
>
> What happened in the meantime was the unexpected return of the absentee landlord whose farms Mr. Isabello and 1,500 other villagers worked. By government order the land was to be converted into a large-scale corporate farm with high-technology equipment to plant sugar for export. Displaced by mechanized farming, the villagers had no choice but to leave the lands—scrambling to eke out a slum existence by driving jitneys or selling clothes.

Amos's description of elite oppression has its lesser, and for the most part obvious, counterpoint in his references to the peasantry. They are most often called the poor and needy (three times in parallelism). They are called the indigent and oppressed, those who have been mulcted and who have suffered extortion. Amos's vocabulary includes a word I've translated "peasant," but he doesn't use that word when describing the ruling class's oppression of the peasantry, probably because it's too neutral. The one initial surprise in the way Amos refers to the peasantry is the first word used, the "righteous." What an offense to those whose socioeconomic status practically forces them to believe that poverty is the proof of wrong.

Even with a knowledge of the societal conditions in Amos's day, the meaning of some lines from his prophecy remains unclear. An example: "The man and his father (who) go to the girl / to profane my holy name." The usual understanding of this line is hinted at by the RSV: "a man and his father go in to the same maiden," as though they had had sexual intercourse with her, a regular meaning of "go in to" in Hebrew. Exod. 21:7–9 suggests the background: "When a man sells his daughter as a slave . . . if [her master] designates her for his son, he [the master] shall deal with her as with a daughter [and so not have intercourse with her]." Amos's concern then, would be the rights of the peasant girl sold into slavery for the relief of her family's debt, and her abuse by her elite master. This is possible, as is some form of forced prostitution for the poor girl, for that matter. But the text doesn't say "go in to," only "go to"; it doesn't say "slave," only "girl"; and it doesn't say "the *same* girl," only "the girl." These demurrals are inconclusive. I strongly suspect, however, that this line does not refer to intercourse with a peasant slave, but rather to an institution known in considerable detail from Mesopotamian documents: the role of the alewife, or barmaid (the "girl"), as broker. A man and his father *must* go (the verb may be translated modally) to the alewife to obtain a loan at exorbitant rates or else a man and his father go to the alewife to invest for a usurious return. Either the man and his father are peasants, or they are the ruling elite. The latter alternative *may* fit better with the succeeding line in the oracle. I prefer the former, which by its mention of son and father seems to allude to the breakdown of patrimonial domain. A law from the Code of Hammurabi suggests the origin of what strikes us (though not persons from other parts of the world) as a strange combination of alewife and broker: "If an alewife give one flask of drink on credit, she shall receive thirty-five quarts of grain at harvest time in return." Drinking on credit can quickly turn a person into a debtor, to the benefit of unscrupulous creditors and their henchwoman. Historians would be quick with their objections to this alewife theory, too. There is no other evidence for this institution in the Syro-Palestinian area, and none at all for it later than the middle of the second millennium B.C., eight hundred years before Amos. Whatever the meaning of the line—abuse of a debt slave, forced prostitution, saloon credit, or some meaning not yet discovered—the principle of seeing it in relation to the overall socioeconomic picture is a sound one.

Revelry. The oppression of the peasantry supports the festivity of the ruling class. In fact, the intensity of the latter is a direct measure of the severity of the former. The more extravagantly the elite revel, the harsher the pain in the peasant's belly. The wasteful consumption of calories by the elite drastically reduces the calories available to the peasantry, whose caloric margin of survival is thin. Debility and disease become widespread. There are other effects of the festivity of the ruling class. Amos bemoans their carelessness in sharp contrast to the desperation of the peasantry. He bemoans the implied reduction of the peasants' own ceremonial fund, essential for maintaining social relationships among the peasantry. And he bemoans the channeling of resources into commodities out of the reach of the peasantry.

The final couplet of the description of festivity—"who drink from ample wine bowls / and anoint with the prime of oils"—corroborates other evidence for this artificial channeling of resources. Some eighty years ago archaeologists excavating at Samaria discovered in a storehouse adjacent to the royal palace (the "stronghold") sixty-five shards inscribed as receipts for shipments of wine and oil (only those two products as far as that storeroom went) from the countryside into the city. The shards date to the time of Jeroboam II or Menahem. Why had the ruling class channeled land and agricultural resources so extensively into these two products, probably at the cost of land for more vital consumables? The terms for wine and oil on the shards hint at the answer: the wine is called "sleeping wine," that is, aged wine, and the oil "oil of washing," oil for anointing oneself after bathing, exactly as in Amos's oracle. These are costly luxuries. The ruling elite in Samaria are clearly among the consumers of these luxuries. But, prodigious topers though they were, they couldn't drink and smear it all. These luxuries were concentrated in the urban storeroom for another purpose as well. They were there waiting to be shipped abroad as durable commodities valuable to members of the ruling class elsewhere in the Near East. They represented one more trade item—in addition to metals, precious stones and woods, ivory work, cloths, spices, and incense—into which the ruling class could transform the surplus of the peasantry in order to bargain on the international market for their security.

But Amos's description of festivity involves more than these general effects. He describes a specific feast, the *marzech* feast. Knowledge about this feast has grown by leaps and bounds in the last decade. A *marzech* was a "sodality devoted to feasts for the dead" (Pope, "Notes on the Rephaim Texts," p. 166). Membership in the *marzech* was limited to the ruling class, mostly men of the military elite but including women. Its chief reason for being was its feast, and an extravagant feast it was. The *marzech* held its feast in a special "*marzech* house," sometimes the lavishly decked house of one of its members, sometimes a house acquired or built for that purpose alone—a sort of fancy clubhouse. The *marzech* house came at times under royal patronage, and the dead for whom the feasts were held included royal departed. The feast was thus held near or at the royal graves. The *marzech* feast (here I contrast the A and B stages) was a party in Samaria for the elite, not a pilgrimage festival in Bethel or Dan joined in by the peasantry. The costs for keeping the house and staging the feast were enormous; some of the extant documents record who is going to foot the inordinate bill.

The trademark of the *marzech* was its notorious drunk.

When they feasted, members expected of one another nothing less than consumption "from ample bowls" to the point of delirium and unconsciousness. According to one Ugaritic text (*Ugar-V*, text 1, lines 15–22), even the god El ends up on the floor:

> El sat at his *marzech* feast.
> El drank wine to satiety,
> Strong wine to drunkenness.
> As El headed for his house,
> Moved off to his rooms,
> [His helpers] picked him up.
> There approached him a "creeper" (he's seeing things)
> With two horns and a tail.
> He floundered in his excrement and urine.
> El collapsed, like those who go down to the nether world.

What a mess. (Compare Isa. 28:7–8.) El, like the rest of any *marzech*, ends up down and out. Indeed, the sodality is named for the consummation of their drunk: *marzech* means roughly the "fellowship of those who keel over." Thus Amos sees them "*stretched out* on garments taken in pledge / drinking the wine of those they mulct," "*prostrate* upon their divans," "*prostrate ones*" whose feast will pass away. The goal of the participants in this feast for the dead was to become, in a paradoxical denial of their own death, like the dead.

And so they shall.

> For Yahweh is about to give the command—
> He will smite the great house into fragments
> And the small house into splinters.

Even royal patronage will not protect the house from Yahweh's war against the ruling elite, announces Amos. You'll not only be "like those who go down to the underworld," you'll go down there with them.

Yahweh's war against the ruling class returns measure for measure. It is a just response, cutting off the elite's power at its wellspring: military might. On Yahweh's day, the day of battle, he will fight not for the military elite, but against them. The confident die. Strong, well-fed, well-armed, and plunderous, they stumble with leaden feet as in a nightmare, or flee in vain into dark and distant corners. Noblewomen call to their husbands for wine, but their husbands are off to the netherworld. The women are raped and slaughtered or left to mourn the dead. The peasant bewails in glee the ravaging of vineyard and field and the utter collapse of the urban market. The house is destroyed, the vineyard pillaged: the mention of house and vineyard together alludes not only to the *marzech*'s extravagance, but also to the builder of the new house and the planter of the new vineyard (Deut. 20:5–6) who might be excused from Yahweh's war, but is not. There are no exemptions. The party is over. Mirthful shouting and song turn into wailing and dirge. None escapes.

GOD AND JUSTICE

Amos's announcement is acute enough to penetrate to the heart of ruling class behavior and simple enough to be reduced to one basic concern: socioeconomic injustice. That is not a new insight. What may be new to some is that it is his *only* concern. Amos deals exclusively with what any human being aware of the rudiments of oppressive societal forms and behavior, or suffering under them, could see. Amos describes the obvious.

But he says "Thus says Yahweh," and Yahweh is not obvious. Why God? What does the mention of God add to Amos's indictment? Can't a person condemn injustice without God?

When taken together, the theological premises that spark Amos's announcement suggest at least a partial answer. There are four such premises. The first premise is that there is *an agent who stands beyond the world who acts in the world* (Yahweh). This agent intends, then speaks, and it happens. God's word is effective not because it is somehow "dynamic" (von Rad), a tempting but needless hypostatization of "word" that severs the agent from his act. It is effective because speaker and agent are one. Amos's words make known God's intent; that God's intent becomes event goes without saying.

To Amos, at least, and *maybe* to his hearers it goes without saying. But to us? Are we to believe there is an agent in the world other than causes and their effects that regress to some unknown or uninformative beginning? The only reason I raise this seemingly trite conundrum is that it makes all the difference in the world. An unjust world governed by cause and effect might just as well remain an unjust world. Amos claims the unjust world is about to be turned on its head. The only way he could really make that assertion is by a faith that God acts in the world. Amos is not a theologian in the sense of one who is going to explore this problem philosophically. His theology follows with little reflection, hard on the heels of his assertive faith.

The second premise is this: *this agent acts according to justice.* Justice means saving the hurt and powerless. Another way to put it: we live in a world ultimately governed by justice, contrary to appearances. Or is it contrary to appearances? Injustice prevails so far, but nearly all human beings would agree justice is better. Israel was related to the one who governs the world justly because Israel was the recipient of that justice: Israel originated in a salvation from powerlessness and so had a covenant with the agent in the world. (Here it is usual to point out the basis of Amos's concept of justice in the Mosaic covenant. This is an old and much debated issue in Old Testament studies. Since Amos does not mention the covenant, it seems appropriate to understand his concept of justice on the basis of the theological principle of justice that the covenant itself rests on. Historically, of course, the covenant may well intervene as the immediate source of Amos's concept of justice, even though there is no direct evidence for this.)

We know justice is better for us than injustice. But then there is a gap: what is better for us in our powerlessness is not necessarily better for others when we are the powerful. The prophets call this gap "to forget," and "to transgress (laws of justice)." Why do we forget? Why do we transgress? Who knows? The most profound treatment of these questions in the Bible is the one given them by the pentateuchal strand called J (Jahwist), but it's just a treatment, not an answer. The point is, we do forget, we do transgress. And that's why Amos requires this second premise: there is one who does not forget justice.

To forget can be fatal. The third premise shows God's

priorities: *the one who acts in the world chooses justice ahead of life.*
Yahweh places his salvation of the powerless before his choice
of the Israelite ruling elite as his people, life for the powerless
before life for the powerful. By now you are aware of how
radical this premise is. It's not the same as what we usually
think of as the "prophetic" mode (the one that critiques) in
contrast to the "constitutive" mode of faith, the one that sus-
tains community (J. A. Sanders, "Hermeneutics," p. 405).
Amos's announcement is not a critique, but a condemnation.
(We will come to the critical mode in stage B.) It is not a
program for reform, but a death sentence. It does not address us as human beings struggling with the question, "What
are we going to do about our forgetfulness and transgression?" Amos does not say that God urges us to help the poor,
or that God will approve our helping the poor by and by, or
that God favors the poor over the rich. What he says is this:
those who take life from the powerless will lose their own
lives. It's that unmanageable. But given that agrarian rent
capitalism and other systems perniciously feed on themselves,
could this premise be mitigated without nullifying justice?

The fourth premise is this: *the one who acts in the world tilts
the balance of power by giving leverage to human beings to make
God's justice known.* God gives Amos the freedom to speak.
This is the closest the A stage comes to dealing with the
authority of Amos. Why God? Is it because without God our
only choice is to make peace with injustice? Is there really an
alternative without God?

Theological language gives Amos and us the opportunity
to talk meaningfully about the revelation of the principle of
justice. It does not enable us to go behind justice to explain
it. The failure of theological language, Amos's or anybody
else's, to explain justice fuses justice and faith. The principle
of justice by which the world is ultimately governed is not a
natural law. To see it is ultimately a matter of faith, not dis-
covery; of deduction, not induction. This shortcoming of
theological language exposes justice as the core of our faith.
And the theological premises beneath the words of Amos
expose it as the categorical but unsearchable core it is. Today
we can and must talk about justice in sociological, biological,

41

psychological, and philosophical terms; to do so is not to explain justice, though it makes it more recognizable here and now. But these ways of talking do not bring us as the people of God to the fundamental nature of justice. Insofar as the use of theological language nowadays risks saying nothing at all (or, even worse, risks using language to muddy truth and justify injustice), the oracles of Amos are a lesson in the use of theological language, God's language itself, that both guards and exploits its limitations.

WHY PROPHESY?

The principle of justice comes to be important to those, including ourselves, who look upon the death of the ruling elite in Samaria. And the fulfillment of Amos's oracles became important as a validation of the principle's truth and Amos's authority. But of what use were Amos's words to his addressees?

None. I want to press this point because it runs contrary to common sense, especially for those whose favorite verse from Amos is "Seek good and not evil." I must anticipate stage B and elaborate for a moment on what was *not* of concern to Amos, namely an improvement in his listeners.

What might give a prophet any authority to influence the powerful or counteract the way they deal with people like Amos, through neglect or worse? There are several ways to tell a prophet without genuine authority (a false prophet), but only one way to tell a prophet with genuine authority (a true prophet): what he says is going to happen happens (Deut. 18:21–22). I don't think there are any other answers, but there are other ways of putting this one. When asked the question, How does one tell a true prophet? at a recent conference, Henri Mottu responded after some thought, "The true prophet is the one closest to reality." What he meant was reality in the sense of actuality, the result, as it were, of God's act. It is truth in the sense of the old English word "sooth," which comes from a form of the verb "to be" and means "that which is."

The reality that Amos is close to is the annihilation of the ruling elite. No one is forced to recognize his authority until that reality happens. As an unvalidated prophet, even if he had wanted to cause his hearers to change, he could not have succeeded. If the annihilation does not occur, his addressees live but do not have to change: "God wasn't angry with us after all; he likes us. It's all in your imagination, Amos." If the annihilation does occur, was it not futile for Amos to waste his breath on the condemned? To think that he prophesied for the benefit of us onlookers is not to take seriously the subject and address of every one of his oracles. Amos's oracles imply no response, have no future, offer no program, and leave no room for repentance. They lead directly to an absolute dead end.

Then why prophesy? Such prophecy seems so futile. From Amos's point of view it is not his prophecy that is futile but the situation he condemns. Two things may be said. First, Amos prophesies the way desperate people speak—with a *cry*. (If he was a stockman [*nōqēd*, 1:1], he may not have been one of the desperate peasantry himself.) The hard-core oppressed of this world are not into urgings, suggestions, programs, reforms, recommendations, or alternatives. The pain of marginal existence drives them directly to a sense of the absolute, the sheer difference between life and death. Oppression produces not a counterprogram, but an outcry. That outcry may be polemical, but it is not calculating or strategical. There's no place for reform as long as there's no recognition of a problem.

In his autobiography William Sloane Coffin tells an incident that illustrates what I'm talking about. Coffin is with a small group selected to deliver a briefcase containing relinquished draft cards inside the Justice Department. One of the three young resisters in the group is Dickie Harris.

> Dickie was not to be hurried. Very slowly, his roving eyes carefully avoiding Mr. McDonough [of the Justice Department], he asked quietly, "Man, are you going to hear me?"
>
> Mr. McDonough look puzzled. "Yes, Mr. Harris. I'm listening."
>
> Instantly Dickie slammed his hand down on the table. Staring straight at McDonough, he shouted, "I didn't say

'listen,' I said '*hear* me,' man." I could see we were in for a fine black rap, probably the first Mr. McDonough had ever heard, let alone experienced with himself the victim. "Yes, Mr. Harris," he said, his face flushing, "I'm listening—I mean hearing. Please continue."

But Dickie was not to be prodded. Slowly he leaned forward, all the while looking intently into McDonough's eyes. Then once again very quietly—until he reached the last syllable of the last word which came out like a cannon shot—he said, "Man . . . you . . . don't . . . ex*ist.*"

McDonough recoiled and actually began to pat himself up and down. Meantime Dickie roared on, "We're going to ignore you, man, you're nothin'." His scorn was magnificent; but after five minutes I interrupted him. "I think Mr. McDonough's heard you by now, Dickie. So let's ask him if he has anything he wants to say to us."

McDonough shot me a grateful glance. "As a matter of fact," he said, "I do have something that I would like to say." Reaching inside his coat he pulled out a typed statement. Clearing his throat he was about to read it when with a great show of offended credulity Dickie leaped to his feet. "Man," he said, "You ain't gonna read that?"

"That was my intention, Mr. Harris."

"Well, I ain't gonna listen. See you cats later." With that he swung himself out of the room (*Once to Every Man*, New York: Atheneum, 1977, pp. 249–50).

It is hard for us to hear the kind of speech represented by Amos's A-stage oracles because it is directed in part against us, because we are so thoroughly socialized to compromise, because we are not familiar with marginal existence on a collective basis, and—though this is a tricky matter—because some of us may at times have adopted such speech largely for its rhetorical effect, thus distorting our sense of its true origin and nature. Like the B-stage editor, we therefore tend to translate Amos's words of condemnation into words of mere indignation. We must instead force ourselves to hear the speech of Amos for what it is. It can help teach us to hear the categorical cry of the desperate for what *it* is.

In the second place, Amos prophesied because he was commissioned to do so. Yahweh called him, told him what to say, and to all intents and purposes left him no choice in the matter. This brings us again to the point where we no longer explain, but simply listen and, if possible, accept.

What about the remnant? Don't the prophets allow a remnant to be saved? I count five different places in the oracles of Amos that bar a remnant, and no place that states there will be a remnant. The six or so passages in the book of Amos that mention or suggest a remnant belong unmistakably to the B and C stages. Might not these go back to Amos, who could have referred to the peasantry as a remnant, preserving the categorical specificity of the oracles to the ruling elite?

I think not, on four grounds.

1. To assign the references to a remnant to Amos violates most of the characteristics of the A-stage oracles.
2. To suppose the elite cared about a peasant remnant, or that the peasantry overheard these references to themselves, contradicts the specificity of the address of Amos's oracles.
3. What would have prevented the elite, furthermore, from latching on to this straw of hope for themselves?
4. The most important consideration is this: the admonition which is invariably part and parcel of the unambiguous references to a remnant has as its purpose to exhort those addressed to change their ways, to give up wickedness in favor of righteousness. But Amos calls the peasant from the start, a priori, the righteous.

It is false to mitigate Amos's announcement with the notion of a remnant. Yahweh will annihilate the ruling elite.

3
Justice and the Scribe: Stage B

What Amos said was going to happen happened. Shalmaneser V captured and sacked Samaria in late summer or fall of 722. Scores of Israelites died in battle. Shalmaneser's successor Sargon II deported 27,290 survivors to distant parts of the Assyrian realm. It is safe to guess that these comprised the large majority of the ruling elite and their artisan dependents. The Samaritan oppressors of the Israelite peasantry condemned by Amos were no more.

In one sense a fulfilled prophecy is like an unused theater ticket the morning after the performance. There's not much to do with it but throw it away. Why weren't Amos's oracles thrown away? The reason is simple but important: in another sense a fulfilled prophecy is an authenticated intelligible report of God's intent, and as such is too valuable to discard. Instead, Amos's oracles were considered so valuable they were preserved and taken to be applicable to times, places, and persons other than the ones Amos so specifically addressed. In other words, they were reactualized, or again made present and understood as having present meaning. This was a momentous yet typical occurrence. It was momentous because without it we would not have the prophecies of Amos. It was typical because it represents what happens many times over in the history of the formation of Scripture: the preservation of authoritative writings and then the necessity to interpret how what was first meant for one group of people later applies to another group. The ultimate results of this process are the Bible and biblical interpretation.

In addition, Amos himself was authenticated. The concept

of author in Israelite society, as throughout the ancient Near East, was different from ours. The authors of the great works contained in the first part of the Bible, including the penta-teuchal strands and the Deuteronomistic History, are unknown to us. Authorship becomes significant when the author claims to be speaking not his own words but God's. The one who transmits God's authentic words is worth identifying.

In this chapter we are interested in how the words of Amos were reactualized in the seventh century, roughly the time from Hezekiah to Jehoiakim, in what I am calling the B stage. The B stage contains basically two kinds of material. The first kind is the A-stage oracles discussed in the last chapter. The second kind is B material. It does not share the characteristics of the A-stage oracles, but has its own set of distinctive characteristics, and it concerns issues known to have been important in the seventh century. Our main purpose in this chapter is to discern the B-stage meaning of this second type of material. We will also have to ask how the A-stage oracles are to be reread in their new context.

What we are calling distinctive B-stage material was composed, not out of nothing, but out of received prophetic traditions. These received traditions go back mostly to the eighth century, probably in part to Amos. I call this material B rather than A because its direct connection with Amos is much less evident than with A material and because it has been recomposed to express meanings quite different from those of the A-stage material. At the end of this chapter we will consider what meaning these B-stage materials had in their original eighth-century context, before they were re-composed by the Bethel editor.

The B stage of Amos differs in some important ways from the A-stage material. It was written. The order of its material thus was fixed, and so it needs to be considered in its present order. (There is no evidence the C-stage recomposition of B had any appreciable effect on the order of B materials.) It was longer, including most of what is now Amos 1:1–9:6, minus a few C-stage additions and variations. The meanings it conveys depend on getting an overview of the entire document and on making connections between sometimes widely separated passages. For these reasons I will present the B stage differently from the way I presented the A stage. First I will discuss the significance of three major themes in the B stage: (1) Bethel, (2) the fall pilgrimage festival *succoth*, or feast of booths, and (3) the prophet. Then, on the basis of the distinctive characteristics of the passages that pertain directly to these three themes, it will be possible to look at the rest of the B material. Finally we will consider the setting of the B stage: who composed it, for whom, and why?

BETHEL

Where Amos A concerned Samaria, Amos B concerns Bethel. Where Amos A concerned a socioeconomic opposition, the cleavage between ruling elite and peasantry, Amos B concerns a religiopolitical opposition, between Bethel and Jerusalem as cult sanctuaries. Where Amos A concerned the *marzech*, the ritual partying of an exclusive sodality, Amos B concerns the *succoth*, the fall national pilgrimage festival. Where Amos A addressed the narrow class of the ruling elite, Amos B addresses the far wider range of people who participate in the *succoth* festival. The basis for all these contrasts is the first, Amos B's interest in Bethel.

Bethel is mentioned seventy-one times in the Old Testament; only Jerusalem is mentioned more often. The key to Bethel's importance is its location. Bethel was a relatively small town situated in the very heart of the central hill country of Palestine, with the hill country of Ephraim stretching some fifty kilometers to the north and the Judean hill country extending an equal distance to the south. Bethel lay on the main north-south road that followed the watershed of the hill country along its entire length, from Shechem and beyond in the north to Hebron in the south. (Dan and Beersheba, two other important sanctuaries mentioned in Amos, marked the farthest northern and southern extremities of the territory regularly inhabited by the Israelites. The location of the Gilgal mentioned in Amos is uncertain.) When the people who called themselves Israel became resident in the hill country as a distinct political entity some two hundred years or so prior to the founding of the monarchic state, they made this central, accessible town one of their chief sanctuaries. It became the place to which a large segment, if not all, of Israel gathered during their three prescribed annual pilgrimage feasts, passover, weeks, and booths, to renew their collective identity and celebrate the main harvest seasons of barley, wheat, and fruits.

Unlike Samaria and Jerusalem, the site of Bethel offered no particular military advantages. Its purpose was to serve, not as a stronghold for a military elite with hegemony over the surrounding countryside (note, however, 1 Macc. 9:50 for a later period), but as a sanctuary and market town whose value to the wider society was predominantly cultic. (I can think of no reason other than its total lack of geographic interest why pictures of the site of Bethel appear so rarely in books about the Bible and Bible lands.) Its ritual activities included offerings and sacrifices, group lamentation, divination, the distribution of contributions in kind to the needy, and, in some way, the recitation of stories of salvation, the purification of the people, the enactment of the theophany of God, and possibly the ratification of a covenant. From early on, resident priests and prophets performed their services there. The altar is thus the local feature most remembered (Gen. 12:8; 35:1,3,7; 1 Kings 12:32–13:5).

At the division of the kingdoms, Jeroboam I sought to establish a cultic legitimation of his agrarian monarchy to rival the monarchic cult of Jerusalem by reviving the cults of Dan and Bethel, which had fallen into disuse during the reigns of David and Solomon. Dan and Bethel were located at the northern and southern borders of his kingdom; Bethel was hard by the very road that led south to Jerusalem. Jeroboam put his mark on these cults, and so turned at least Bethel into what Amos could call the sanctuary of the king, by reverting to apparently venerable bull statues to counter the keeping of the ark in Jerusalem (see Judg. 20:26–27), gathering a new priesthood from representative parts of the kingdom, and moving the celebration of the fall pilgrimage festival, the feast of booths, one month later.

The cult of Bethel continued to function even after the fall of Samaria in 722. The Assyrians repopulated Samaria with a replacement ruling elite imported from far and wide but retaining their accustomed social class and function in their new locale. Little changed for the peasantry. They were still forced to deliver their surpluses to the new elite in the form of rents, taxes, duties, fines, and other exactions. The new Samarian elite maintained the cult of Bethel to help legitimate not only their socioeconomic control over the countryside but also their enforcement of Assyrian imperial policies. Although some of the peasantry apparently fled to Judah, most remained in their former homes and condition and continued, along with people from other segments of society, to attend the periodic festivities at Bethel.

As the Assyrian empire was collapsing 100 years later, Josiah broke loose from beneath its yoke and attempted to recreate the dominion of David and Solomon. A key feature of his program was the centralization of power and authority throughout the greater Israelite territory in the temple of Yahweh in Jerusalem, the temple that Solomon had built. In pursuance of this policy Josiah tore down the altar of the sanctuary at Bethel and incorporated the town and its environs into the administrative framework of the kingdom of Judah. There is no evidence that the cult of Bethel was ever restored.

As is commonly recognized, the deuteronomistic historian took Josiah's destruction of the altar at Bethel to be the ultimate vindication of the altar in Jerusalem. It permanently validated the house of Yahweh in Jerusalem, built by Solomon at the height of Israelite dominion, against the pretension of the counter-house-of-God (*beth-el*) revived at Bethel during the schism. The singular importance of Bethel from the deuteronomistic point of view is evident from these two familiar passages from the Deuteronomistic History:

> Jeroboam instituted a pilgrimage feast on the fifteenth day of the eighth month to duplicate the pilgrimage feast in Judah. As they sacrificed on their altar, so he did in Bethel, sacrificing to the bulls he had made. When he had stationed in Bethel the sanctuary priests he had appointed, he made sacrifice upon the altar he had made in

Bethel, on the fifteenth day of the eighth month, which he had arbitrarily appointed as a pilgrimage feast for the Israelites. And as he ascended the altar to light the sacrifice, there appeared a man of God who by the word of Yahweh had come from Judah to Bethel. Just as Jeroboam was about to light the sacrifice, the man cried out against the altar by the word of Yahweh, "O altar, altar! Thus Yahweh says: 'A child is to be born to the house of David, Josiah by name, who shall sacrifice upon you the sanctuary priests who burn incense upon you and who shall burn human bones upon you. And he shall perform a sign in that day' "—he described it in these words—"this is the sign that Yahweh has spoken: the altar shall be torn apart and the ashes upon it spilled about" (1 Kings 12:32–13:3).

Likewise the altar at Bethel, the sanctuary instituted by Jeroboam son of Nebat, who made Israel sin [through worship of the bull at Bethel], likewise that altar and sanctuary [Josiah] tore down and broke up until they were fine dust. Then Josiah turned and saw the graves there. He sent someone to get the bones from the graves and had them burned upon the altar, and so defiled it, according to the word of Yahweh that the man of God cried out (2 Kings 23:15–16).

Why does Josiah destroy the altar at Bethel? Because he has found the Torah document, consisting of at least Deuteronomy 12–28, in the temple and committed himself and his people to carrying out its stipulations. The document's *primary* stipulation is for the one single people to worship Yahweh, the one single God, in one single place:

The place which Yahweh your God chooses from all your tribes to set his name there, for his dwelling, (that place) you shall seek and there you shall enter in (Deut. 12:5).

As becomes clear in the course of the Deuteronomistic History, that place turns out to be Jerusalem. Thus the Deuteronomist presents the ruination of the cult at Bethel as the result of—even the *paradigm* of—Josiah's carrying out the law that limits the cult of Yahweh to Jerusalem.

With this background concerning Bethel, let's look now at what the book of Amos says about it.

> On the day I assail Israel for their transgressions, *I will assail the altars of Bethel*: the corners of the altar will be hewn away and fall to the ground (3:14).

* * *

> *Enter in at Bethel, and so transgress*
> At Gilgal, and transgress greatly
> Present your offerings the (following) morning
> Your tithes on the third day
> Send up your thank offerings with unleavened grain-cakes
> And loudly proclaim your votive offerings
> For that's the way you "love" (me), O Israelites—
> oracle of the lord Yahweh (4:4–5).

* * *

> Seek me and live
> *Do not seek Bethel*
>   Nor enter in at Gilgal
>   Nor pass through to Beersheba
>   For Gilgal will go into exile
> *And Bethel will become nought.*
> Seek Yahweh and live, lest he burn the house of Joseph as with fire, and (the flames) consume, and there be no one to put them out, *on account of Bethel* (5:5–6).

And where *is* Yahweh to be sought, if not at Bethel? The B stage provides the answer to this question before it even arises, in the exordium, the first prophetic words:

> Yahweh roars *from Zion*
> *from Jerusalem* he bellows.

Yahweh is in Jerusalem, so don't go to Bethel. The opposition of Jerusalem and Bethel was a seventh-century issue, as the Deuteronomistic History makes clear. Was it also a concern of Amos? That seems doubtful. When Amos condemned the Israelite elite for transgressing God's law, he was appealing to standards of justice the northerners would, in theory anyway, recognize as valid. They at least paid lip service to the law of God and its relief of the powerless. But to instruct them not to go to their national shrine Bethel, a venerable Israelite center of worship whose traditions reached back to the very beginning of Israelite presence in the hill country, and by implication to go to Jerusalem, would have been to appeal to a tradition, Yahweh's choice of Zion, that had little or no validity in the northern kingdom. Or more to the point, the appeal would be to an issue of great importance in the southern kingdom after the fall of the north. As we have seen, the cult at Bethel was not effectively stopped, if it was stopped at all, following the exile of the Israelite elite. Moreover the language of Amos 5:5, "Do not *seek Bethel,* nor *enter in* at Gilgal," is similar to the language of Deut. 12:5, *"The place* which Yahweh chooses you shall *seek,* and there you shall *enter in,"* in that the verb "seek" takes an object of place only in these two passages and in 2 Chron. 1:5 (in the latter likewise in reference to the temple built by Solomon). As will appear later on, the structure of the B-stage document makes this opposition of Jerusalem and Bethel unmistakable. We may infer that the view in Amos B that Yahweh's cult in Jerusalem precludes the cult of Bethel is akin to the deuteronomistic view that Yahweh is to be worshiped in Jerusalem alone, and that it does not come directly from the prophet Amos.

SUCCOTH

The Bethel editor's particular interest shifts from the private party of the ruling elite, the *marzech,* to the national pilgrimage festival attended by a wide selection of the populace, *succoth. Succoth* provided the occasion for celebrating the culmination of the entire agricultural year, a frequent subject in the B stage. The gathering of the harvested grain had been completed by midsummer. During the summer the various fruit crops—particularly grapes, figs, olives, and pomegranates—gradually ripened, and by the time of *succoth* their ingathering was fully under way. *Succoth* was likewise the time for the production of new wine, and the festival often developed the character of a bacchanal. Anticipation ran high that the coming agricultural year would be as productive and plentiful as the previous one. This was the time when the drought of the hot summer months was about to be alleviated by the beginning of the rainy season. And if the longed-for early fall rains had already begun, there was all the more reason for celebration.

We can best begin to see the role of *succoth* in the B stage by looking at its conclusion. There the B editor has framed an A-stage oracle by means of a vision of Yahweh beside an altar before the oracle and a description of Yahweh's appearance, or theophany, after the oracle. I have put the B-stage frame in italics.

> *I saw the Lord stationed by the altar, and he said,*
> "Smite the topstone so the thresholds quake
> Slash away at the heads of all of them
>   Every last one of them I will slay by the sword
> Not one of them shall flee
>   Not one of them shall escape
> If they grovel into Sheol
>   From there my hand shall take them
> If they go up to the sky
>   From there I will bring them down
> If they hide on the top of Carmel
>   From there I will search out and take them
> If they hide from my sight on the bottom of the ocean
>   From there I will command the snake, and it shall
>   bite them
> If they go into captivity with their enemies behind
>   From there I will command the sword, and it shall
>   slay them
> *And I shall set my eye against them for evil, not for good"*
> *The Lord Yahweh of hosts*
> *Who touches the earth and it melts*
>   *And all who dwell in it fade*
> *And the whole thing rises like the Nile*
>   *And settles again like the Nile of Egypt*
> *Who builds his upper chambers in the sky*
>   *Who founds his . . . upon the earth*
> *Who summons the waters of the sea*
>   *And pours them out upon the surface of the earth—*
>   *Yahweh is his name* (9: 1–6).

The B stage thus ends at the doomed altar as the earth quakes. This quaking at the end is the same quaking that is referred to at the very beginning of the B stage, in its heading: "The things that Amos saw for two years before the *quaking*" (1:1). The difference between A and B in the conclusion is quite apparent. The A-stage oracle describes the futile flight of warriors from the scene of battle, as in 2:14–16. The B setting makes this same oracle into a description of people fleeing in fear from an earthquake. It introduces this description with a prose sentence and follows it with another using the vague words "evil" and "good"—the B stage is typically more prosaic and vague than the A stage.

Yahweh appears as the one who shakes the whole earth by making it rise and fall "like the Nile." He is the one who builds storehouses for rain in the sky, chambers for the oceans above that pour down on the earth when the windows in the sky are opened. Since he built their storage chambers, he is the one in a position to summon the waters of the new rainy season.

But will he summon them? Does the quaking that breaks into the heat augur good rains or not? The images used to describe the theophany of Yahweh are ambiguous. The quaking is as much a warning as a destruction: the inhabitants of the world "fade" in the heat, a fate distinctly less severe than death, just as the lushest highlands "fade" at the withering blast of Yahweh's roar:

> Yahweh roars from Zion
> From Jerusalem he bellows
> The shepherds' pastures *fade*
> The top of Carmel withers.

When the Nile rises and falls (end of summer, beginning of fall), it floods the earth with needed water and leaves it more fertile than before. Yahweh is the one who controls the cosmic waters that descend as rain and flow up from the deeps into the streams that refresh the land. He can cause a destructive flood or a restorative watering. Will the quaking be for us or against us? That is the question that is left open, again typically, by the B stage.

It is likely that the descriptions of Yahweh here and in 4:13 and 5:8–9 make use of the tradition of theophany at the pilgrimage festival. For those in attendance, the theophany doubtless represented an unqualified blessing. The B editor, however, is concerned to maintain the intrinsic ambiguity of Yahweh's appearance, the ambiguity that made possible Amos's caustic ironies about the "day of Yahweh." Yahweh can appear against his people as well as for them. Which one he will do depends on their response.

Whether for us or against us, in either case the earthquake reduces the sanctuary and altar to rubble. In the B stage these can be none other than Bethel's sanctuary and altar. Not unexpectedly, the crisis represented in B (we will discuss it shortly) reaches its greatest intensity at the altar at Bethel.

The B stage arrives finally at Bethel for good reason: it has come round to the time of *succoth*. The B editor makes clear that two years have indeed passed prior to the final quaking. He does this by means of two sequences, in 4:6–13 and 7:1–9:6. Each has five parts suggesting a seasonal progression, each culminates in the time of *succoth*, and each concludes with a description of the appearance of Yahweh.

The first year is marked by a sequence of five events taken as warnings. The seasons are readily identifiable. Nine months or so from the previous grain harvest, in midwinter, the grain, and thus the bread, run out. From then to the normal time for the wheat harvest, the spring rains, which are necessary if famine is to be avoided, fail. Blight takes hold in the vineyards and orchards in early summer. A pestilence strikes the king's army campaigning in midsummer, when under normal conditions they could have expected the roads to be passable and food along the way plentiful. Finally the people are "turned," a vague expression often used of Sodom and Gomorrah, and they become like a glowing brand rescued from the "burning": the late summer heat feels like the fire God rained on Sodom and Gomorrah. An explicit but ambiguous threat, "For this I will do to you," ends the first year.

The second year is marked by a sequence of five visions in 7:1–9:6. The bit of hay that sprouts for the peasantry after the king's mowing of the primary crop is threatened by a locust swarm in late spring. When summer comes, an unusually intense heat wave threatens to parch the orchards and vineyards. The vision of the plumb (if that is what the obscure word *anak* means) is not recognizably seasonal. However, in the scene that intervenes between this vision and the vision of the ripened summer fruit that follows, Amos says that he is a dresser of figs. He apparently refers to summer work analogous to what the Gezer Calendar, an early Hebrew doggerel naming the agricultural seasons in order, calls "dressing vines" and places at this time. Then the ripened fruit is gathered at the end of summer. The collective word for "summer fruit" sounds exactly like the word for "end," and on the basis of this pun Amos B brings the sequence to the brink of disaster. At this critical point, the prophet, along with his readers, metaphorically joins the throng congregated to celebrate the gathering of the fruit, in the feast of *succoth*, at the altar at Bethel. And Yahweh comes, too.

What then is the significance of *succoth* for the B stage? *Succoth*, we have said, is a culminating time. It is also a time that comes on the boundary between the end and a new beginning. Nights are becoming longer than days. The life-giving rains are about to begin again—maybe. The harvest of one year is completed and the plowing and sowing for the next are about to begin—maybe. It is a critical time: the total harvest of the previous agricultural year can only now be assessed, while the initial conditions that will affect the following year's production are just about to become apparent. *Succoth* is thus the B stage's primary metaphor for the ultimate moment of critical decision (compare Jer. 8:20; Neh. 8:18), as in the deuteronomistic work (Deut. 31:9).

But *succoth* has another more specific significance for the B stage. It was during *succoth* that Solomon transferred the ark to the newly built sanctuary of Yahweh in Jerusalem, and all the people of Israel gathered to dedicate it (1 Kings 8:2,65). Likewise it was during *succoth*, as we have seen, that Jeroboam I sought to dedicate the reinstituted cult at his rival sanctuary at Bethel (1 Kings 12:32–33). Since *succoth* commemorates the dedication of both rival sanctuaries, there is no better moment to represent the conflict between them. *Succoth* symbolizes the opposition of Jerusalem and Bethel.

It is unlikely that the understanding of *succoth* in the B stage goes back directly to Amos, since it involves making literary interconnections that span the entire length of the B-stage document.

THE PROPHET

We saw in the last chapter that Amos's inexorable sentence of death precluded a response. At least no response was called for and no obvious, expected way to respond was left open. The oracles of the B stage do expect a response. Along with the narrative that goes with them, they urge and warn, and therefore require a hearing, a decision, and obedience. In fact, for the B stage *the* basic transgression is the wrong response to the prophetic warning. All other transgressions stem from one: the refusal to hear and obey. According to Amos B, Jeroboam the king and Amaziah the priest of Bethel refused to hear Amos or even to allow him to speak, and *that* was the cause of the "end" of the northern kingdom. Whatever other transgressions the people may have committed, when the prophet appears to urge them to "turn," as the B stage, like the Deuteronomist, puts it, all previous actions fall under the shadow of the final test, their response to the prophet.

Jeroboam and Amaziah spurned Amos. *That* was what immediately brought on their own end. But in the B stage their end is only penultimate. Their end took place in the past and serves as the primary example of a similar test now. The B stage continues on, beyond the spurning of Amos at Bethel. It draws out the end. It keeps open the critical moment, maintains the challenge, faces present readers with the continued choice of whether to heed Amos, and urges them to respond.

We can outline B's view of the role of the prophet by citing a skeleton of key passages in order.

a. Yahweh roars (as a lion) from Zion
   From Jerusalem he bellows (1:2).
b. You ordered the prophets, "Do not prophesy" (2:12).

c. Does a lion roar in the forest if it does not have a prey (3:4)?

d. The Lord Yahweh does not do anything unless he has revealed his counsel to his servants the prophets.

> The lion has roared
> Who will not fear?
> The Lord Yahweh has spoken
> Who will not prophesy (3:7–8)?

e. Then Amaziah the priest of Bethel sent to Jeroboam with these words: "Thus says Amos, 'Jeroboam will die by the sword, and Israel will go into exile from off its land.' " Then Amaziah said to Amos, "Do not prophesy at Bethel anymore." But Amos answered, "Yahweh said to me, 'Prophesy.' Since you say 'Do not prophesy,' therefore you will die on unclean ground, and Israel will go into exile from off its land" (7:10–17 shortened).

f. The end has arrived (8:2).

These passages are not haphazardly scattered throughout the B stage, but occur at important points in it: *a* is from the exordium, which serves as the opening statement of all three major themes of the B stage; *b*, from the B-stage insertion in 2:9–12, is the culminating offense in the oracle in 2:6–16 (thus not only in 7:16–17 but also in 2:12–13 the B editor hangs the "therefore" directly on the spurning of the prophets); *c* and *d* represent the climax of the first of three major blocks of material in the B stage; and *e*, marked by a change from first to third person, is placed in the center of the series of five visions in 7:1–9:6, immediately prior to *f*, the vision of the "end," the key position of which speaks for itself and epitomizes B's view of the role and function of the prophet. And we are not surprised to notice that the B editor places Amos's *decisive* encounter with his opponents not in Samaria but in Bethel.

In the B stage the prophet's role is to warn people that Yahweh is roaring mad. Both the A and B stages picture Yahweh as a lion, but they are readily distinguishable. The A stage pictures Yahweh as a tearing, killing lion and uses the word *ari* (3:12; 5:19). The B stage pictures Yahweh as a roaring, warning lion and uses the word *aryeh* (3:4,8, both with "roar" as in 1:2).

The B-stage view of the prophet's role in the fall of Samaria is essentially a version of the Deuteronomist's:

> Because the Israelites sinned against Yahweh, built for themselves sanctuaries in all their cities, and, when Yahweh warned them by every prophet, every seer, saying, "Turn from your evil ways and keep my commandments and statutes in accordance with the entire set of stipulations which I imposed upon your ancestors, and which I sent to you by my servants the prophets," they did not listen, (for these reasons) Yahweh became very angry with Israel and removed them (2 Kings 17:7,9,13, 14,18 shortened).

The prophet warns. Catastrophe results from the rejection of the warning and the spurning of the warner as much as from the transgression itself. To heed the warning is to avert catastrophe. To spurn the warning is to invite catastrophe. Amos announced the inevitable application of the curses in Deut. 28:15–68. The B stage *re*offers the crucial choice of Deut. 30:19: "I have set before you life and death, blessing and curse; therefore choose life, that you and your descendants may live." If an event described in Deut. 28:15–68 should occur, as several do in Amos 4:6–11, it is a warning rather than a final curse. For Amos, God has chosen. For the B stage, the people are to choose. For Amos, God chose curse because the people had chosen transgression. For the B stage, the people's choice is open again. Amos bound a future to a past. The B stage focuses squarely on the present. Whereas Amos said in effect, "You have not set justice in the gate; therefore I will destroy you," the B stage says, "Set justice in the gate" (5:15).

There are further hints of the similarity of the B-stage passages mentioned in this section to the deuteronomistic tradition. The B editor capitalizes on the coincidence that Jeroboam II has the same name as the founder of the monarchic Bethel cult. In light of the possibility discussed in the previous chapter that Amos did not prophesy during the reign of Jeroboam II, he may even have created the coincidence. The description of Bethel as "in the midst of the house of Israel," if it is not merely figurative, seems to conceive of Israel in terms of the reuniting of the northern and southern territories attempted by Josiah, a program for which the Deuteronomist served as chief theorist. Some have suggested that the "man of God from Judah" in 1 Kings 13 was modeled on Amos, in the kind of literary allusion we are more and more aware the biblical writers were adept at making. The lions in 1 Kings 13:20–32 and 2 Kings 17:25, cropping up so curiously to both kill and warn and at precisely these critical junctures, may be related to the B stage's portrayal of Yahweh as a lion.

The prophetic documents produced during the century from the time of Josiah to the end of the Babylonian exile all contain a scene, or several scenes, like the one in Amos 7:10–17. The prophet's audiences invariably ignore, spurn, silence, persecute, injure, or even kill him. This scene is invariably linked with the prophet's call, since his call substantiates the claim of authority which is the most offensive thing about the prophet from his persecutor's standpoint. This scene is invariably linked with the prophet's intercession, for himself or others, when it is present. And it invariably comes to represent the turning point as it is conceived in a prophetic book, the point where the prophet's condemnation shows itself to contain the clues to its own reversal, if only the hearers will "turn." In Amos as in other prophetic books, then, the drama of the spurning of the prophet imbues the entire book, providing the rationale for Yahweh's anger and destruction as well as the rationale for the hope that Yahweh could relent.

Amaziah's response to Amos raises the issue of the readers' response. Amos disappears from view—where he goes or what happens to him is intentionally not told—and the spotlight shifts to Yahweh and then out onto the readers. No prophet comes back on stage, victorious or vindicated, to take his final bow as God's effective messenger of justice. The kinds of prophets that were validated by the experience of exile in both north and south were not the kind that were ever well-received by their hearers. Literarily, it would be premature to the B editor's intent to resolve explicitly the spurning of Amos by telling how he survived his confrontation with the authorities at Bethel. The prophet, after all, would return victorious only after his hearers, or readers, had allowed his warnings to sink in and take their effect, "turned," and adopted the program of justice he had urged. But that has not happened yet. The fate of Amos is left hanging, as is the fate of every other prophet, because the fate of the prophet at his hearers' hands is the *issue*, not the answer. That is, the B editor's intent is not to announce that the prophet has been obeyed, but rather to raise the issue as sharply as he is able: now that the prophet has spoken, or been recorded, what are you going to do? How are you going to respond to Amos? The fate of Amos is left hanging because the fate of justice is only now to be decided.

DISTINCTIVE FEATURES OF AMOS B

Even the few passages from the B stage seen so far allow us to draw up a list of distinctive features of the B stage in Amos which contrast with the distinctive features of the A stage listed in the previous chapter.

1. Whereas Amos A addressed a specific and limited audience, the B stage addresses a *general audience*. Usually they are not even described. When they are, it is in relatively vague terms like "those who turn judgment to wormwood and who leave justice on the ground" (5:7). Amos B addresses three groups: people who remained in the north following the Assyrian invasion; the people of the south in general; and the ruling elite in the south. That's specific enough, except that it involves virtually everyone in the society. We will have more to say about two of these three groups and how Amos B speaks to them near the end of this chapter.

2. Amos A proclaimed a single basic message: exile and death for the ruling elite. The B stage has a different basic message, with various elaborations: *perform justice or else.*

3. Like the oracles of Amos A, the oracles and other materials of the B stage share among themselves a set of stylistic features, many of which set them off against the A-stage oracles. Whereas by far the largest portion of Amos A is poetic,

B-stage material is marked by a great deal of *prose* and *prosing of poetry*. Here it is necessary again to caution you that most English translations give a false impression of the quantity of poetry in the book of Amos. You will already have noticed that several of the lines quoted so far in this chapter as prose appear as poetry in your translations. We will have to be attentive to this important, though not absolutely determinative, feature as we seek to discern the B-stage material. The B stage sometimes repeats the same word instead of using a parallel term (examples: "house" 3:14–15; 5:4–6; "families" 3:1–2; "assail" 3:2,14; "transgression" 4:4). B-stage phrases tend to be *wordy* rather than terse, *vague* rather than specific, *abstract* rather than concrete, and *stereotyped* rather than fresh. In other words, while Amos A was likely to call a spade a spade, the B editor would just as soon call it an instrument or implement. In the B stage one does not "sell the needy into debt slavery for a pair of sandals"; instead one "does wrong." There is ultimately no specific, authoritative rationale for the pro-Jerusalemite stance; so the B editor calls it, in effect, "good."

The language of the B stage may spring largely from liturgical rites. It tends to be vague the same way church language tends to be vague. Mic. 6:8 is another good example of a dictum modeled on liturgical speech. When my colleague in Old Testament and I were asked recently to prepare a fresh translation of Mic. 6:8 for our seminary catalogue, we spent a lot of time trying to figure out how to make its abstractions as concrete as possible. Finally we copied the abstractions. They weren't meant to be concrete, but to cover as many different people as attended the rite. Love good, not evil—let the hearer fill in the particulars. The B editor of course includes some particulars, for example in the A-stage oracles.

4. The B stage shows every sign of being a _written composition_ rather than oral. Some have surmised that it may even have been promulgated along with the first, or Josianic, edition of the Deuteronomistic History (so-called Dtr 1) as part of a major literary production, although it is also possible there was an earlier collection of Amos oracles put together

during the reign of Hezekiah or Manasseh. I know of no way to tell whether it utilized a written or oral collection of the oracles of Amos A. The B stage was intended to be read, exactly as composed, by or to its audience. It represents a simultaneous collection, preservation, promulgation, and actualization of the oracles of Amos A.

5. Whereas the oracles of Amos A speak directly and eschew ironic reversals, the oracles and narratives of the B stage are careful to *maintain ambiguity*, ironically if need be, in order to keep open the choice that they offer in the end.

6. As in the A stage, the forms of the B stage enhance meaning; thus the B-stage *forms tend to imply open-endedness*. The B-stage counterpart of the judgment speech is the prophetic *rib*, the "suit" or "litigation," which is both demanding and open-ended. Other forms found in the B stage include chastisement, exhortation, call to worship, the narrative describing the commissioning of the prophet, the speech in the divine council, prophetic visions, and theophanies. Several of these may have their original setting in the Bethel cult. There are passages whose forms are difficult to specify, including larger organizational units, probably because the form criticism of strictly literary forms, those pertaining for example to the prophetic collection, is a neglected area of Old Testament study.

It is in the B stage of Amos, not the oracles of Amos himself, that one finds almost all the forms characteristic of "wisdom" tradition described by H. W. Wolff in his book *Amos the Prophet*. Scholars have recently renewed their interest in the relationship of "wisdom" to the deuteronomistic tradition. Their conjunction in Amos B occasions no surprise given that both "wisdom" and the deuteronomistic tradition derive in their present forms from the scribal circles of the urban ruling elite in Jerusalem near the end of the monarchic period, where the arts of writing and literature were practiced and controlled.

7. Whereas in Amos A the meaning of an oracle was self-contained, in the B stage *meaning is often dependent on juxtaposition or placement within a larger whole*. Amos B consists of three

major extended units, or blocks of material, 1:2–3:8, 3:9–6:14, and 7:1–9:6. Within these blocks are other long units with extraordinary climaxes, such as 4:6–13, and complicated structures, like 5:4–15. The B editor prefers sequences of five—why is not known. (I have wondered whether this preference for five might build a typical B-stage meaning out of "For three transgressions . . . and for four . . . , " and still one more, a fifth, chance.) Sequences of five occur at least four times within the largest units. The point for the moment is that the B editor intends meanings which depend on making connections across the relatively long distances of extended units.

8. In contrast to the A stage, the B stage offers an *open future*, a new possibility, and, ironically, a virtually perpetual crisis. One can state this openness in any number of ways: warning, chastisement, discipline, exhortation, admonition, instruction, or even "wisdom."

9. Exhortation *cannot*, by its nature, *be fulfilled*. The fulfillment of exhortation would be justice itself; there is no sign that human society has run out of the need for more. Since fulfillment cannot be at issue, the authority for exhortation cannot be grounded in exhortation itself. In other words, unlike the prediction of catastrophe, the command "Do justice" does not have within it the basis of its own authority. That is one reason why it is linked as it is to the story of a prophet whose authority *is* very much at issue in the narrative.

In all these ways, then, the B stage of composition shows itself distinguishable from the A stage. Again, what makes the analysis cogent is what makes the analysis of the Pentateuch into strands, or any other literary analysis of the Bible, necessary: the consistent grouping of characteristics which pertain *as a group* to a given set of passages.

THE B-STAGE CORPUS

Let's now turn our attention to the B-stage material, particularly the parts not yet examined. This discussion will be selective, though detailed enough in some places to clarify points that are not readily apparent in translation alone. The structure of the B stage, with its three major blocks of material, can be sketched as follows:

	1:1–2	Heading and exordium.
I.	1:3–3:8	Five warning oracles from Jerusalem.
II.	3:9–6:14	Five groups of oracles against Bethel.
III.	7:1–9:6	Five warning visions at Bethel.

Keep in mind that the B editor intends the reader to read the interspersed A material also; we'll return to that toward the end of this chapter.

1:2–3:8 FIVE WARNING ORACLES FROM JERUSALEM

We have already seen, in the discussion of the B editor's view of the role of the prophet, how 1:2 relates to 3:3–8. This section will presume that discussion and concentrate on 1:3–3:2, which the B editor regards as one long roar from Yahweh. In what sense is this so?

You have no doubt heard many times about that viciously sardonic speech Amos once made to the assembled crowds, vain in their nationalistic self-satisfaction. If you have ever preached on this passage, you may have talked about it yourself. One after another Amos names nations bordering Israel, and one after another he denounces them. As each fresh victim succumbs to Yahweh's wrath, the glee of the Israelites grows ever more intensely fervent, until suddenly Amos turns on his immediate audience and condemns them no less than the nations whose downfall they so recently and recklessly cheered. Then the sword falls: "Hear this word that Yahweh is speaking against the *whole* family whom I brought up from Egypt . . . you only have I known . . . therefore I will assail you . . . . "

Did this speech really occur? There are admittedly some reasons to believe it did. Its irony is like that of Amos. The genre of the individual oracle against a foreign nation may have had its original setting in the service of the military elite, Amos's exclusive addressees, and thus the ironic use of this genre was predictably most effective with that group. The sentence, "I shall not cause it to return," is suitably categorical to be attributed to Amos. Amos 6:2 indicates that Amos did keep an interested eye on international affairs (though many have argued, not implausibly, that this verse is secondarily added). Some of the incidents seemingly referred to in 1:3–2:3 can, with a degree of success, be related to ninth- and eighth-century events. An oracle against Aram makes historical sense only before 732, when Damascus fell to Assyria.

But there is also evidence for believing this speech did not occur as so described, at least in anything like its present form. The oracles which definitely go back to Amos suggest that he did not require such a long hearing or the making of connections over such an extended amount of material to make his points. He was adept at achieving equivalent irony in much briefer scope. It is important to recall that the one other possible grouping of this sort in the identifiable oracles of Amos, the mention of "Ho! Ho!" in one oracle (5:16) followed immediately by two more oracles each beginning with "Woe!," serves to dissolve Amos's irony rather than create or reinforce it. The precedent is a poor one. Amos did not denounce the *whole* people of Israel through the judgment in 2:6–16, an oracle that in any case stands on its own in the A stage. The address to the *whole* family fits the B stage much better. The B stage is also addressed in part to the military elite, so that one of the best reasons for linking these oracles with Amos does not necessarily limit them to the A stage. Historians are uncertain whether the smaller nations in these oracles conducted wholesale deportations as a military or political strategy, especially in the eighth century, during most of which it was not even an Assyrian policy. As we shall see, not only do these oracles represent a set, but a special set of five, a number that links them to at least two other groups of five in the B stage. The vaguer language of the final lines of this section (3:1–2) is typical for the B stage.

In its present form, 1:3–3:2 is a *C-stage* composition. The first task is to discern its B-stage dimensions and wording.

This is easier than might at first appear. The main point is to bracket the oracles against Tyre, Edom, and Judah at this stage. To see why that is necessary, let's look first at the oracle against Aram.

> Thus says Yahweh:
> For three transgressions of Damascus and for four I shall not cause it to return—
> (1) Because they threshed Gilead with threshing sledges barbed with iron pegs,
> > I will send fire against the house of Hazael
> > And it will consume the citadel of Ben Hadad
> (2) And I will break the bar of Damascus
> > And cut off the enthroned one from Biqat-Awen
> > And the one who wields the scepter from Beth-Eden
> > And the people of Aram will go into exile to Qir
> (3) Says Yahweh (1:3–5).

We are interested in how the *form* of this oracle differs from the one to be considered next, since that's how the C-stage editor allowed it to keep its distinct identity. Notice, therefore, three items: (1) the indictment is a single transgression, stated in prose; (2) the sentence includes more than the first two lines concerning fire in the citadel; and (3) the oracle concludes with "Says Yahweh." Note also that, like the B stage as a whole, this oracle singles out the monarch for special culpability. Now read the oracles against Philistia, the Ammonites, and Moab and notice how they are like this oracle against Aram. Together they form a group of four.

The oracle against Tyre is different.

> Thus says Yahweh:
> For three transgressions of Tyre and for four I shall not cause it to return—
> Because they delivered Edom into a total exile
> (1) *And did not remember the covenant of brothers*
> > I will send fire against the wall of Tyre
> > And it will consume her citadel (1:9–10).
> (2,3)

Notice the three ways it differs from the four oracles just

named. The indictment is expanded and stated in semipoetic lines; parts 2 and 3 are missing. The oracles against Edom and Judah are like this oracle against Tyre. In chapter 4 it will become clear why these three are assigned to the C stage.

We are now in a position to outline the B stage of this section. For this purpose it is not necessary to translate the oracles in their entirety, but simply to note their positions and similarities.

> Yahweh roars from Zion (1:2)
>
> Oracle against Aram (1:3–5)
> Oracle against Philistia (1:6–8)
>
> Oracle against the Ammonites (1:13–15)
> Oracle against Moab (2:1–3)
>
> Oracle against Israel (2:6–16)
>
> Hear this word which Yahweh has spoken against you, O Israelites, against the whole family whom I brought up from the land of Egypt: "You only have I known of all the families of the ground—therefore I will assail you for all your iniquities" (3:1–2).
>
> When certain things happen, it is a warning that something else is sure to follow (3:3–6).
>
> Yahweh does not do anything unless he has revealed his counsel to his servants the prophets.
>> The lion has roared
>> Who will not fear? (3:7–8)

Note the pairing of the oracles by means of similarities between the first two and the second two, leaving the last standing by itself. One meets with the same characteristic pairing in two out of the three other series of five in the B stage.

The B editor conceives of two sets of warnings here. The first set is addressed as though to northern Israel: after four warnings Israel is condemned, because it is known to have failed to heed Amos's warnings. Since Assyria is not included among the indicted nations, it is clear the B editor has in mind the historical setting of the fall of Israel. A second set of warnings applies to the B audience directly. These are five warnings, including the fall of Samaria itself, against "the Israelites, the whole family whom I brought up out of Egypt," that is, the entire audience of the B stage. It can happen to you too, Judah, as to these five. It is characteristic that the B-stage audience gets *five* warnings, *one more* than hitherto. The idea that Amos pronounced the oracles against the nations to trap a crowd of cheering Israelites in their vainglory is a modern interpretation with no basis in the text.

The B-stage style of this first major block is represented by several phrases and features. A number of deuteronomistic cliches occur: "all your iniquities," "through his servants the prophets," and particularly the fivefold "I will not cause it / them to return," with its repetition of the Deuteronomist's favorite word "turn," to suggest that these warnings—that you will be exiled if you do not repent—are dire indeed. The parade of examples here is similar to the parade of example nations across the stage in the very beginning of the Deuteronomistic History (Deut. 1–2), nations whose individual histories foreshadow and exemplify Israel's taking of the land. The vaguer language of the B stage is evident in the many general, stereotyped, and repeated phrases of this section. Not the least of these are the repetitions in the oracles against the nations, unique to Amos and needing an explanation.

Originally the oracles against the nations may have functioned, in the cult of Bethel, like other B-stage materials, as part of its nationalistic celebration of Yahweh's military victories on behalf of all the assembled people. Of this we cannot be sure. The surprising placement of the oracles against the nations at the beginning of the document rather than at some more obvious turning point is not characteristic of exilic collections of prophecies, to judge from parallels in other prophetic books. The indication is, therefore, that the C editor inherited this order from the B stage, where it originated.

2:8–12. The B editor has made an insertion at 2:8–12 that modifies the thrust of the original oracle of Amos in 2:6–16 considerably. In so doing he brings the indictment against

Israel to a culmination with the spurning of the prophets, the B editor's distinctive way of summing up injustice. The entire insertion reads as follows (part of A-stage original in italics):

> *Who stretch out on garments taken in pledge* near every altar
> *And drink the wine of those they mulct* in the house of their
>   god
> Though I destroyed the Amorite before them—
>   Whose height was like the height of cedars
>   And strong was he like the oaks—
> And I destroyed his fruit above
>   And his roots beneath
> And I brought you up from the land of Egypt and
>   caused you to walk in the wilderness for forty years
>   to possess the land of the Amorite
> And I raised up some of your sons as prophets
>   And some of your braves as Nazirites
> Is this not the case, O Israelites?
> Yet you forced the Nazirites to drink wine
>   And you gave the prophets these orders:
> "Do not prophesy."

There are good reasons why these lines are to be regarded as a B-stage insertion, besides their view of prophecy. The B-stage additions to the first two lines make them too long for normal poetry. The syntax of the rest is prosaic, with some parallelistic phrasing. The phraseology is deuteronomistic: "Amorite" for the pre-Israelite inhabitants of Canaan, "to possess the land of," "raise up prophets," and "bring up" from Egypt in this context. Amos A does not use the broad phrase "Israelites."

This insertion is more than just another reference to "exodus tradition." It integrates the three particular concerns discussed at the beginning of this chapter. That is, it refers to the spurning of the prophet during the festival of *succoth* at Bethel. The two additions "near every *altar*" and "in the *house of their god*" (compare "the *altars* of *Bethel* [house-of-god]" 3:14) are triggered by the reference at the end of the A-stage indictment to the drinking of wine, a primary activity at the festival of *succoth*. In the A stage, this would have referred of course to Samaria; now it is made to refer to Bethel. The entire insertion is thus framed by festival wine drinking at one end and forcing Nazirites to drink wine at the other end. (To force the Nazirites to break their vow to Yahweh is to spurn the counterauthority which their vow represents; this is analogous to spurning the prophet's commission from Yahweh; compare the juxtaposition of Jeremiah 35 and 36.) Lev. 23:43 suggests that the forty years in the wilderness alludes to dwelling in booths, or *succoth*, during that time.

The insertion achieves its effect in part by allusion. The comparison of the Amorite to cedars and oaks alludes to a particular form of exodus tradition in which Israel is compared with a vine. This tradition is best exemplified by Ps. 80:8–11:

> You moved a vine out of Egypt
> > You drove out the nations and planted it
> You prepared the ground for it
> > It rooted well
> > And filled the land
> The mountains were covered with its shade
> > The great cedars with its branches
> It sent its roots as far as the subterranean sea
> > Its root strands as far as the underworld river.

Whether the Amorites are displaced or overgrown, the vine Israel flourishes in their place.

Another way this insertion refers to drinking wine at *succoth* is based on the association between the insertion and the scene in which Amaziah spurns Amos:

> You gave the prophets these orders: "Do not prophesy" (2:12).

> Do not prophesy against Israel
> > And do not *drip* against the house of Isaac (7:16).

What does "drip" mean in this context? "Preach" is not a bad translation, but it does not explain why a word that usually means "drip" is used. This word is still commonly thought to refer to the drooling of ecstatic prophets—a very doubtful derivation. The truth is that it is used here metaphorically. There are two closely related kinds of dripping, and both can metaphorically mean "advise." The *first* kind pertains to hands or lips dripping honey, myrrh, or wine. (The word is used in this sense in Amos 9:13.) The connection between the dripping of wine and prophecy as the "dripping" of advice is disclosed by the dialogue of a confrontation similar to Amos's with Amaziah, in Mic. 2:6–11, whose beginning and end read as follows:

> "Stop *dripping* [prophesying]!" they *drip*
> "Let them [the prophets] not *drip* about these things"...
> If a man came in the spirit [inspired/intoxicated] and lied deceptions—"I *drip* for you in wine and beer!"—*he* would be the "*dripper*" [prophet] for *this* people.

The *second* kind of dripping pertains to clouds or sky dripping water. The connection between it and advice is disclosed by Job 29:21–23:

> They listened to me and waited
> And kept silence for my counsel
> And after my word they did not speak again
> When upon them my word *dripped*
> They waited for me as for the rain
> Their mouths they opened wide as for the spring rain.

To refer to prophecy as dripping is thus to refer to its instructional value, as in the B stage (compare Deut. 32:1–2) but not the A stage. The association that the insertion has, through 7:16, with the concept of "dripping" results in this implication: to spurn the prophet is to reject one kind of "drip" (advice) for another (wine). Or, as Micah puts it, the spirit for spirits.

3:9–6:14 FIVE GROUPS OF ORACLES AGAINST BETHEL

You may find the literary subtleties that have so far come to light impressive or—perhaps more likely—bewildering. The B editor would take either reaction as a compliment. The B editor is a literary master: the authority of his work in his own eyes is measured in part by its dazzling array of devices. But does he really expect anyone besides himself to notice them? I imagine he's like some authors (maybe most of us) who think that those among their readers who are qualified to understand will understand. With the B editor, however, this is not a case of intellectual elitism providing an excuse for a tired imagination, but rather an essential expression of the social status that accompanies his office as scribe in the service of the ruling elite. Only an accurate perception of the purposefulness with which he employs literary devices can enable us to recognize their social function.

But to answer the question: does he expect anyone to be qualified to recognize his literary devices? I think the answer is yes. At the same time, it is necessary to make a distinction between two kinds of devices, one more readily noticeable than the other. The more noticeable are the kind we have just been looking at. They depend simply on a knowledge of the language and its connotations. A modern scholar has to struggle to achieve such knowledge, but any ancient native speaker possessed it as a matter of course. These are the kind of devices one could hear with one's ear. They have to do mainly, though not exclusively, with the subject matter. They are accessible to everyone. The less noticeable devices depend on a command of literary conventions far less widely known in ancient times, and on the ability to *read*. They depend on having the document in hand and being able to look at it and study it. They have to do mainly with patterns and structures. When used by the skilled, they often get too complicated for the ear, unless we greatly underestimate the ability of the ancient ear to pick up features we need to study with the eye for a long time to notice. I doubt we underestimate the capacity of the common ancient ear. Rather, this second kind of device is meant precisely for the eyes of those who would have access to the documents—the scribal class itself.

In this section we concentrate more on structural devices, without neglecting the first kind. The central block of the B stage, 3:9–6:14, consists of five pairs of alternating units. The units in one set concern Samaria and those in the other Bethel. The units alternate in the following manner:

Samaria (stage A)		Bethel (stage B)
3:9–12	(1)	3:13–15
4:1–3	(2)	4:4–13
5:1–3	(3)	5:4–15
5:16–20	(4)	5:21–27
6:1–7	(5)	6:8–14

The sharpest boundaries are marked by the beginnings of the Samaria units. The repetition of the phrase "Hear this word" in 3:1, 4:1, and 5:1 impressed the medieval scholar who made up the chapter divisions, but apparently it plays little role in the present schema. Within the units there is some mixing of A and B materials, but the basic outline holds. The theophany in 4:13 also loses the structural significance sometimes assigned to it, while the theophany in 5:8–9 becomes more significant than is usually supposed. It is the nucleus and pivot point not only of this section, but also of the entire B document. Before we come to that, however, I want to comment on some of the purposes of the B editor as he selects and arranges the A-stage oracles, and identify some of the distinctive features of the B stage, unit by unit.

One facet of B's plan for these five units can be discerned immediately: the selection of materials to go into them. He deploys his most distinctive and explicit references to Bethel first, and as he progresses through the units his material gets less explicit about Bethel. This can be seen just by reviewing how the successive units refer to Bethel:

1. I will assail the altars of Bethel: the corners of the altar will be hewn away and fall to the ground (3:14).
2. Enter in at Bethel, and so transgress (4:4).
3. Do not seek Bethel . . . Bethel will become nought (a vague expression based on wordplay) (5:5).
4. I spurn your pilgrimage feasts (5:21).
5. ———

He thus arranges his material so that what is less distinctive and explicit can be read in light of what is more so. By the time he gets to the fourth and fifth units, their specifically B-stage component becomes more difficult to recognize but their B-stage meaning no less clear.

3:13–15. The A-stage oracle in 3:9–11 represents Yahweh speaking to his council in the sky. This council was referred to in 3:7, since the word for *counsel* (RSV, "secret") there also means *council*. The B editor thus joins the two major blocks, 1:3–3:8 and 3:9–6:14, at their cusp by means of a dramatic picture that illustrates his most important point about the prophets: through the prophets, Yahweh intends to reveal the deliberations of his council before he carries them out, in order to warn the people. So he commands these several heralds, among whom is Amos, with *plural* imperatives, "Proclaim . . . and say . . . !" This address to the heralds continues in the first B unit, again with *plural* imperatives: "Hear and warn . . . (about the destruction of Bethel at *succoth*)!"

What distinctive features of the B stage are recognizable? The subject of Bethel, the general audience, and the warning are obvious ones. All but the last two lines are prose. (Again, I can't help feeling how hard it is to convey the weight of this point as long as English translations print all the lines as poetry.) Vague expressions include "assail" (RSV, "punish"), "transgressions of Israel" (Amos A would have named them and their perpetrators), and "smite." The wordy phrase "Lord Yahweh, God of hosts" occurs in an only slightly shorter form in 4:13, 5:27, and 6:14, all in the B stage (Amos A usually makes do with "Yahweh"). The oracle repeats "assail," "altar," and "house," the latter six times, comparable to its fivefold repetition in 5:4–6, another B oracle.

Some phrases might go back to Amos A. "Houses of ivory" is a poetic phrase akin to "couches of ivory" in 6:4 (compare 1 Kings 22:39). Its parallel "many houses," vague though it is, recalls the parallelism of "large house" with "small house" in 6:11, which may go back to Amos. It is not surprising that the phrase "houses of ivory" occurs in one of the two poetic lines. The phrases "winter house" and "summer house" might also go back to Amos A. They have more than one meaning, however. Amos could have meant them to refer to winter and summer residences, although they wouldn't both be at Bethel. They also mean, and could be translated, "autumn storehouse" and "late summer (*qets*) storehouse," both at Bethel. This is their meaning in the B stage, and thus in the oracle as presently composed. The mention of a "late summer storehouse" initiates the seasonal sequence that will culminate with the shaking at *succoth* in the fourth and fifth visions two years later. Amos's main concern was to condemn the people who lived in fine houses. The B editor more than Amos condemns the houses themselves—the people who lived in them can come to Jerusalem.

4:4–13. The call to worship at Bethel repeats the vague "transgress" with the colorless "transgress greatly." By itself "love" is vague, or at least depends on deuteronomistic tradition (there is no "to do" in the text); it is comparable to "love" in the exhortation "love good" in 5:15, likewise from the B stage. There are also some good poetic phrases.

The series of five events arranged according to seasons interprets categorical curses of the type found in Leviticus 26 and Deuteronomy 28 (some of the wording is identical) as warnings, punctuated by repeated chances to repent. The events are subdivided by form and language into a 2-2-1 grouping, like the five oracles against the nations and the five visions. Again like those, they use stereotyped expressions, for instance the refrain, "And you did not return to me—oracle of Yahweh." This refrain employs the deuteronomistic "return" and resembles a remarkably similar refrain also repeated five times and used as a literary device in Isaiah 5:25, 9:12,17,21 and 10:4: "For all this his anger has not (yet) returned." These warning events culminate in what would be, were it not in the B stage, an oddly vague way of referring to the intense heat of summer: "I *turned* you as God *turned* Sodom and Gomorrah."

The call to worship and the series of futile warnings eventuate in the dangerous theophany hinted at by the final stanza:

> Here is the one
> Who shapes mountains and creates wind
> Who discloses to human beings what he has in mind
> Who turns dawn into darkness
> Who strides upon the heights of the earth—
> Yahweh God of hosts is his name.

Together the call and theophany show similarities to Exodus 19 and 20, where the Israelites prepare to encounter God at Sinai. This scene is itself influenced by liturgical reenactment, possibly at Bethel.

> Yahweh said to Moses, "Go to the people and consecrate them today and tomorrow, and let them wash their garments. Let them be prepared on the third day, for on the third day Yahweh will descend in view of all the people upon Mount Sinai. . . . " And he said to the people, "Be prepared on the third day . . . . " (Exod. 19:11–15).

God appears then, inspiring terror:

> When all the people had seen the thunder and lightning and the sound of the warning horn and the mountain smoking, the people were afraid and quivered . . . . And Moses said to the people, "Do not be afraid, for God has come to test you, so that you will not sin" (20:18–20).

The intent of the theophany in Amos B is precisely the same. Yahweh's ultimate act is frightening, but ambiguous, and pointedly unexpressed. Just what is the gesture that goes with the words, "Therefore thus will I do to you, Israel; because I will do this to you, prepare to meet your God"? The B editor wants to leave the future open for one more chance to repent.

5:4–15. Chief among the B-stage features of this unit are its vague exhortations: "Seek good and not evil so that you may live"; "hate evil and love good." When students first read Amos, they often choose these lines as their favorites. I explain to them that they haven't met the prophet Amos until they begin to see vivid, distressing pictures of human misery in addition to these righteous truisms that depend on deuteronomistic tradition for their specificity. These exhortations are addressed to anyone—anyone, that is, who has not yet made the pilgrimage to Jerusalem a habit, who possesses the wherewithal and influence to affect other people's lives, or who holds the social position to make legal decisions. The same general audience is the target of the open-ended qualifiers "lest" and "perhaps." These are inconceivable in stage A, which knows no extenuation and no remnant. This section refers to prophets as B conceives of them: the "chastiser," the "one who speaks of innocence" (i.e., "Seek good and not evil"), and the "prudent one" who finally falls silent, or silenced, in the "evil time."

Given our modern world view, most of us understandably fail to recognize that the theophany in 5:8 is not simply a general description of God the Creator, but a specific description of the God who controls the fall equinox and the return of the rains. For a long time I took "who made the Hyades and Orion" (for the B stage a missing poetic parallel member is not troublesome) to signify the feat of creating stars. I should have asked, why *these* stars? In Hebrew cosmology the stars are one source of rain, with rain thought of as innumerable drops of water dripping through innumerable holes in the sky. The Hyades (Greek "water stars") and Orion are constellations that rise high in the sky at sunrise near the autumnal equinox. They are thus the cosmic harbingers, if not the cause and source, of the rainy season. And God is *their* creator. "The one who turns darkness into morning and darkens day to night" is not, as I had again long thought, simply the creator of day and night, but the one who controls the equinoxes, making nights shorter in the spring when the rains stop, and days shorter in the fall when they return.

The structure of 5:4–15 is significant and requires elaboration. The unit looks like something of a jumble; 5:7 and 5:9 have usually struck readers as being out of place, and in 5:10–13 an A-stage oracle is rearranged and interspersed with B-stage lines. But there is order in this apparent disorder: J. de Waard has plausibly suggested that the unit is an elaborate chiasmus. Chiasmus is a crossing, or inversion, of two members with parallel structures:

> Down came the rain,
> and the corn shot up.

This inversion can be conceived as ring composition, or a series of frames within frames,

> Down came the rain, and the corn shot up.

composed of the corresponding members down–up, came–shot, and rain–corn. The frames can also be represented vertically:

> **Down**
>
> came
>
> the rain,
>
> and the corn
>
> shot
>
> up.

When de Waard discovered the chiastic pattern in 5:4–15, he didn't know *why* it was used here, since he did not relate it to the design of the entire book. For him it was just something fancy that was worth noticing for the sake of a more accurate translation.

It is now clear why the B editor used chiasmus here. Chiasmus is the perfect form to choose for the *center* unit of the *center* section of the entire B-stage document: it provides a framework around the nucleus of the document, setting it off and suggesting a pivot point where the reader turns the corner, as it were, from the first half to the second. This kind of chiasmus is known to have been employed by biblical composers, as in Isaiah 2–12, but its use is not predictable. How is the reader supposed to know it is coming? The B editor signals his intention to use it by composing a minichiasm as an opener:

> Seek me and live
>
> Do not seek Bethel
>
> Nor enter in at Gilgal
>
> Nor pass through to Beersheba
>
> For Gilgal will go into exile
>
> And Bethel will become nought
>
> Seek Yahweh and live.

In other words, the first of the chiastic members is itself a chiasm, expanded by the prose "lest" clause. To print this as though it consisted of conventional pairs of parallel lines obscures its true structure. Not only is chiasmus particularly appropriate to this unit and signaled by its opening member, but also the editor has selected the A-stage oracles on either side of the unit in such a way as to add an additional pair of framing members and thus corroborate the chiasm in between:

> Hear this word which I raise over you in lamentation:
> The virgin Israel has fallen down—
> No more to rise
> She is left abandoned on the ground—
> No one to raise her (5:1–2).

> Therefore thus Yahweh says:
> In all the squares there shall be wailing
> And in all the streets they shall say, "Ho! Ho!"
> (5:16).

The "therefore" in 5:16 in effect follows 5:1–3 rather than 5:14–15.

The chiasmus in 5:4–15 can be perceived by looking for corresponding members as you read toward the middle from both ends. There's no difficulty in spotting the first correspondence, between 5:4–6 and 5:14–15, including the clauses beginning with "lest" (5:6) and "perhaps" (5:15). Next, 5:7 stands by itself ("you" is not necessarily in the text). There are similarities between this line and 5:10–13, and some translations and commentaries have even shifted its location to 5:10. But the line is not out of place, at least for the B editor. He intentionally placed it where it is to create the second chiastic correspondence, between it and 5:10–13. The third correspondence has as its first member the theophany in v. 8. Here again, there seems to be a line out of place, v. 9: in terms of form, either v. 9 belongs in the theophany, or "Yahweh is his name" belongs after v. 9. Why have the positions of v. 9 and "Yahweh is his name" been reversed? The reason is evident: to position v. 9 as an opposite chiastic member and create the third chiastic correspondence, between v. 8 (excepting "Yahweh is his name") and v. 9. Although the first word in v. 9 is obscure, the meaning of the line is clear enough to see that a corner has been turned: the ambiguity inherent in the theophany has been resolved in favor of "destruction" (a vague word, repeated), an allusion to the destruction of the altar at Bethel in 9:1.

The result of the chiastic form is to isolate "Yahweh is his name" at the nucleus to function as the solitary pivot point. The B editor has modeled the larger chiasm and the smaller opening chiasm after each other: three sets of paired members and a single center member. He has also chosen to center his entire document and to end it with the same phrase, "Yahweh is his name," in both places preceded by the same description of the God who appears in order to summon the destroying or fertilizing rains:

> Who summons the waters of the sea
> And pours them out upon the surface of the earth—
> Yahweh is his name (5:8; 9:6)

These lines occurring at the exact center and the very end of the document intentionally answer to the opening exordium of the B stage: Yahweh's roar causes the drought; his summoning of the waters can end it.

By now you may be protesting that it's so artificial! That's precisely the point. It is intended to be magnificently artificial, devised by learned ingenuity to practice the secrets, affirm the values, and undergird the status of a limited and somewhat exclusive class of scribes who had the skill, motivation, and opportunity to pass on the prophetic voice in writing. One must marvel at even the implication that a reader is supposed to keep all of this in mind at once (though once perceived, it becomes increasingly familiar). One must marvel also at the doggedness of generations of scribes who copied this material with relatively little attempt on their own part to straighten it all out according to different literary norms. At the same time, it is necessary to investigate more than has been done the lives and function of this class of writing scribes in ancient Israel and put them in perspective in relation to the rest of society. I will touch on this matter briefly at the end of this chapter.

What about the mixing of A and B materials in 5:7,10–13, which in itself does not bear on the chiasmus just discussed? The sorting out I suggest here is tentative, but it hints at what the B editor is up to. The oracle included in the selection of A-stage oracles in the previous chapter is given on the left, the B-stage material on the right. The B editor has rearranged the A-stage oracle by removing the middle pair of lines from their original context to provide some specific examples of "transgressions" and "sins"—a sure sign that even the B editor thought those terms were a little vague!

A	B
	Those who turn judgment to wormwood
	And leave justice on the ground
	Hate the chastiser in the gate
	Abhor the one who speaks of innocence—
[Therefore]	
Because (they) levy excessive rents upon the poor	
And take exactions of wheat from them	

<table>
<tr><td align="center">A</td><td align="center">B</td></tr>
</table>

Who attack the righteous, who
  take a bribe
And so shunt aside the needy
    in the gate

The fine stone houses you have
  built—
You shall not dwell in them
The delightful vineyards you
  have planted—
You shall not drink their wine

                         Since I know that many are your
                           transgressions
                           And numerous your sins

Who attack the righteous, who
  take a bribe
And so shunt aside the needy
    in the gate

                         Therefore the prudent one in
                           that time will fall silent since it is
                           an evil time.

Changes in person are not irregular. The B column can be
read by itself: because the unjust transgressors refuse to heed
the chastising prophet, he will be silent on the day "evil"
overtakes them.

5:21–27. This unit begins with a poetic oracle that at first
condemns in a style and manner reminiscent of the A stage.

I hate, I spurn your pilgrimage feasts
  I will not smell (the sacrifices of) your assemblies
    [unless you offer sacrifices to me]
  Your offerings I will not accept
    Your fatted covenant sacrifices I will not observe.

Continuing in A-stage style, the lines switch to command and exhortation, as in the B stage.

> Remove from me the commotion of your songs
> The playing of your harps let me not attend
> Let (right) judgment roll like the waters
> And justice like a stream that runs all summer.

Finally the style becomes prosaic and wordy, with vocabulary typical of B.

> Did you [you did—no question] bring near to me sacrifices and offering in the wilderness for forty years, O house of Israel, or bear (this line is corrupt) . . . your gods which you made for yourselves? I will take you into exile beyond Damascus, says Yahweh [the God of hosts is his name].

(Later scribes produced the three changes in brackets. The first was necessitated by a literalistic understanding of "I will not smell your assemblies," with its poetic ellipsis of "sacrifices." The second one, a different vocalization of the same Hebrew consonants, brought the text in line with a different interpretation of the authoritative story of the wandering in the wilderness in the Torah. The third seems to be an expansion based on 4:13.)

More than any other passage in Amos, this poetic oracle mixes the categories proposed in this book in a way that precludes analysis into more than one stage. Nevertheless, it may go back to Amos in something like its present form, a possibility to be explored at the end of this chapter. The B editor has recomposed this oracle slightly and placed it here because it concerns *succoth*. It explicitly mentions pilgrimage feasts and then limits these to *succoth* by referring to the critical return of the rains in the phrases "the waters" and "a stream that runs all summer." The people look for rain. Yahweh looks for justice.

But the B editor wants to condemn Bethel, not *succoth*, and the poetic oracle doesn't mention any place. Therefore he adds the prose conclusion. The corrupt line appears to refer to two idols in apposition to "your gods which you made for yourselves" (compare Jer. 7:21–8:3). It thereby links the spurned festivities to the deuteronomistic "sin of Jeroboam at both Bethel and Dan (1 Kings 12:29–30). If the last line, "I will take you into exile beyond Damascus," is a fragment of a judgment of Amos A, then it once referred categorically to exile in the Assyrian realm. In its present B-stage setting, however, it conveys a warning: I will take you into the desert, where you won't find animals or grain for sacrifices or the rain you are looking for, to teach you a lesson. There is no "therefore." The place is suitably ambiguous, if not vague: "(somewhere in the desert) beyond Damascus," not too far from Dan. The B editor has apparently included Dan in his reference to idols because of the specific mention of Damascus, far to the north of Bethel, in the line possibly from Amos A.

6:8–14. The B editor is running out of good material that says by itself what he wants to say. If he had composed this unit on the basis of a well-preserved oracle of Amos or from scratch, it would, I think, show more coherence and design. There are mere traces of a design. The whole unit is framed by the repetition of "oracle of Yahweh, God of hosts." "House" is repeated five times near the beginning, as with the first and third Bethel units. The suspension of the word "nation" reinforces the cadence of the final line. Either the B editor's ingenuity has given out, or else the material he is employing has turned intractable.

It is difficult to dispel the impression that the B editor has gleaned the isolated lines, phrases, and fragments of sayings he couldn't use elsewhere and stowed them here in the back porch of his schema. The result is his least effective composition, to be read in the light of those that are clearer.

Two of the fragments he uses might come from Amos A. One I have already hesitatingly identified as belonging to stage A in the previous chapter:

> For Yahweh is about to give the command—
> He will smite the large house into fragments
> And the small house into splinters.

Even this fragment is suspect by virtue of the colorless

phrases "large house" and "small house." The second possible A-stage fragment uses some vivid images, including the bitter plants starved peasants resort to eating.

> Do horses run on craggy cliffs?
> Does one plow the sea with oxen?
> Well, you have turned judgment to a poisonous plant
> And the fruit of justice to wormwood.

The bitter plant metaphor is nearly identical to 5:7, from the B portion of the third Bethel unit. It is difficult to decide whether it generalizes injustice or not. The argument in terms of kind—as horses have nothing to do with crags, justice has nothing to do with bitter plants—recalls the evaluation of unnatural combinations in Deut. 22:9–11. In fact, the argument here in Amos is strikingly reminiscent of one of the examples: "You shall not plow with an ox and an ass together" (Deut. 22:10). This reduces injustice to a violation of natural law in a way that strikes me as too abstract to belong to the A stage. On the other hand, the fragment is dramatically in touch with peasant oppression (compare 2 Kings 4:38–41) and addresses the elite in terms of both the customary distinctions the peasantry value and the legal niceties the elite can afford. There certainly are ambiguities in assigning it to either the A or B stage. Whatever its origin, the B editor includes it here because it connotes idolatry, and thus misdirected worship, in deuteronomistic fashion:

> . . . lest there be amongst you a man or a woman or a clan or a tribe whose heart turns this day away from Yahweh our God to go serve the gods of those nations, lest there be amongst you a root that produces a poisonous plant or wormwood (Deut. 29:18).

Matters of style rule against even the possibility that any other lines in this unit derive from A-stage sources in their present form. Verse 8 is categorical enough for A, but some of its phrases are like those in the oracles against the nations, and the parallelism of "hate" and "abhor" occurs also in 5:10, again from the B-stage column in its present form. Verse 9 is an odd, perhaps partially corrupt, prose fragment that seems to treat a remnant as a positive irony, as though it were an optimistic extension of the B-stage addition in 5:3:

> If ten men remain in one house, and they die, and his uncle . . . lifts him to take his bones out of the house and says to whoever is in the far reaches of the house, "Is there anyone still with you?" and he says, "No . . . . "

Even after those ten men die, there is still one left back there in the house who somehow, like the B-stage audience, escaped. And he, terrified like the B-stage audience that Yahweh might appear once more, is told, "Hush! Now's no time to mention Yahweh's name!"

Verses 13–14 consist of a prose fragment composed at least in part by the B editor. The suspension of the object "nation," already mentioned as a possible hint of B-stage design, is rhetorically extreme and contrary to Amos's compact style: "For I am about to raise against you, O house of Israel—oracle of Yahweh, God of hosts—a nation . . . ." "Oppress" is less specific, and less dire, than Amos's terms for punishment.

Some have argued that Lo-Dabar and Qarnaim are the towns in Gilead with those names. The phrase "From the entrance of Hamath to the brook of the Arabah" reproduces almost identically the description of the borders of the kingdom of Jeroboam II at their greatest extent from the Deuteronomistic History (2 Kings 14:25). The content of vv. 13–14 thus has obvious affinities with the A stage. But the prose style precludes calling it A-stage material. As long as it is unlikely, furthermore, that Amos prophesied in the reign of Jeroboam II, the literary allusion to 2 Kings 14:25 belongs with Amos 1:1 and 7:10 as a probable expression of the B editor's concern with worship at Bethel. For the B editor, Lo-Dabar means a "no-thing," an idol, and Qarnaim "two horns," Jeroboam I's bull idol (from the deuteronomistic viewpoint) at Bethel. Thus "the horns we got for ourselves" are no different from "your god(s) which you made for yourselves" in 5:26.

7:1–9:6 FIVE WARNING VISIONS AT BETHEL

Except for inserted A materials, almost all of the third major block in the B stage is prose. Like the first and second blocks, the third consists of a series of five, having like the first a 2-2-1 grouping: a pair of visions with intercession, a pair with wordplay (*anak*, *qets*), and a single one at the altar. The events in the visions function as warnings, like the oracles against the nations and the events in 4:6–11. The seasonal sequence from vision to vision is matched by a spatial sequence. Yahweh is getting closer and closer. During the first year and a half, as it were, in the first two blocks of material up to 6:14, Yahweh is located in his council in the sky above Zion, threatening to descend to Bethel. With a personal appearance at the altar at Bethel as his ultimate goal, he descends to the fields in the first two visions, stands by a wall in the third, approaches the sanctuary storehouse in the fourth, and arrives at the altar in the fifth. Again like the oracles against the nations, the fifth vision is set off from the preceding four by a significant change in form ("I saw" rather than "he showed me") and the inclusion of an essentially unmodified segment of A material. By now you yourself can identify numerous other B-stage features throughout this section.

The narrative reports of the third block raise an historical question of some interest and importance. Since these reports seem so personal and biographically precise, do they come directly from the prophet Amos? Do they tell accurately what really happened to him? Instinct says yes, and instinct may have a part of the truth. A majority of redaction critics suppose that three kinds of material in the prophetic collections go back directly to the prophet: poetic sayings, first-person reports by the prophet, and third-person reports about the prophet. The prophetic books do tell different stories about the prophets, and it is reasonable to assume that their distinctiveness has some basis in biographical fact. It is also safe to assume some nearly self-evident generalizations: Amos sympathized with the peasantry and probably appealed to God on their behalf, and anyone who said the things Amos said is going to be called mad, accused of conspiracy, ostracized, thrown out, beaten, or worse. These reports are accurate, at least in terms of these generalizations. By itself, however, without a literary analysis and assessment of these reports, the historical question of whether they accurately report specific, unique events that happened to Amos can only be answered in uncertain terms: something like this probably happened to Amos.

The literary question enables us to be more precise. To what in the book of Amos are these reports most directly related? The answer is unambiguously the B stage, contrary to the majority view. That literary certainty prevents us from saying simply that they go directly back to Amos, but it also provides a basis for differentiating what are distinctive B-stage concerns from what might represent authentic biography. The elements in these reports that contradict what is known from the A stage probably do not go back to Amos. The elements that contribute to B-stage concerns (these include most of the salient features of these reports) are *ambiguous* evidence for Amos's biography. The specifics left over, like the name Amaziah, probably represent historical remembrances going back to Amos, or at least to a time prior to the B editor. The reports look genuine, but from the literary critical perspective their genuineness must be tested in each detail. The reason for being initially skeptical is to give ourselves the opportunity to ask the literary question prior to the historical question.

It is worth asking why these reports should raise for us an historical, biographical question without being able to give a certain answer to it. The reason is that we have momentarily mistaken the literary nature of the reports, and therefore what issue they primarily involve. In effect, this puts the historical question before the literary question. To us the reports look very much like journal entries, and so we assume they are dealing with an issue that in our experience journal entries deal with: what happened to Amos. But we have begged the literary question. To consider these reports as journal entries is implicitly, but without literary analysis, to put them in the A stage and to understand the issue they deal with to be what happened to the Amos who pronounced oracles of judgment against the ruling elite in Samaria. But is that where they belong literarily, and is that the issue with which they are dealing? The literary question that has been ignored will not go away. Why are these reports totally geared into the most distinctive B-stage passages in the book of Amos, into nothing less than the rhetorical basis of the book? Literary analysis makes clear that the issue dealt with in *these* reports is, to get to the root of it, what happened to the Amos who heard "Yahweh roar from Zion, two years before the shaking." Or, to put it less metaphorically, the issue is "Will you, my seventh-century readers, heed the warning of Amos or not?" This issue pertains not to Amos but to the Bethel editor. It is an issue raised by his own situation, needs, and presuppositions. He deals with it *possibly* by using traditions going back to Amos, but *certainly* by deriving salient ingredients from his own experience, including the medium of literary composition. The point is not that these reports do not accurately report what happened to Amos, but that we cannot be certain they did. The reason these reports cannot give a certain answer to the question of what happened to Amos is that they are not journal entries composed to deal with that issue, but historical fiction composed to deal, in their present form, *exclusively* with a different, seventh-century issue. That is the certain result of asking the literary question prior to the historical question.

The First and Second Visions. The first vision, and the second to a lesser degree, vividly portray the precarious balance between life and death in which the peasantry, the "small" ones, struggle for subsistence. To this extent they accurately reflect the condition of the peasantry during much of Palestine history, including the time of Amos. The particular events themselves were ones to which the peasantry in Amos's time were pathetically vulnerable.

Yet it is doubtful that in the visions' present wording and B-stage context the speaker is the Amos of the A stage, or that Jacob here is the peasantry. The speaker begs, "Forgive!" Jacob has thus by implication already been found guilty. But Amos A held the peasantry to be "righteous," and therefore not in need of forgiveness. The innocence or guilt of Jacob is again at stake in the second vision of Yahweh's "litigation" with fire. Again the speaker's plea is not that Jacob is innocent, but that Yahweh should relent (in his anger).

Who then is this B-stage Jacob whose plea must be for clemency rather than of righteousness? There may be a clue in the first vision, which involves a two-stage event. The first is the king's mowing. This represents an oppressive act of the kind that Amos regularly denounced. Where is Amos's anger at this act of the ruling elite? Or Yahweh's, for that matter? The second stage is the devastating swarm of insects—a natural disaster. About *this* the speaker makes his appeal, and Yahweh responds, "*It* shall not be." In Amos A that is Yahweh's response to the ruling elite. Here it is his response to a natural disaster, albeit one exacerbated by the elite. (Notice that it is typical for the B stage to tie the natural world explicitly into God's system of justice.) Why do the ruling elite, at least until the narrative gets to the individuals Amaziah and Jeroboam, appear to get off the hook? Once again we perceive the B editor appropriating traditions of relief in favor of the peasantry and adapting them to give the ruling elite one more chance. That chance could be secured through God's clemency. As the B editor understands him, Jacob represents those who elsewhere in the B stage are exhorted to "hate evil and love good." They are persons who have positions and power to influence justice. In other words, Jacob is himself in part a segment of the ruling elite.

The Third and Fourth Visions. As Yahweh nears the altar at Bethel, the B-stage meanings intensify. The important ones have already been discussed. A few that might not otherwise be apparent call for comment. The visions involving wordplay are by nature ambiguous. Whatever an *anak* (RSV, "plumb line") is, the wordplay created probably means either "I am about to set *myself* (*anoki*) in the midst of my people" (a reference to Yahweh's theophany at Bethel) or "I am about to set *you* (implying an ungrammatical form with *-ennak*) in the midst of my people." The latter instantly happens: Amos appears in Bethel to pronounce his final warning and be spurned. Either represents an event whose outcome per se is ambiguous, to be determined by the readers' response.

The issue of Amos's authority comes to a head in his encounter with Amaziah. The very question of whether Amos was a "prophet," still discussed by scholars as a question of grammar even though H. H. Rowley effectively put it to rest decades ago, contradicts the whole point of the passage. Of course he is a prophet. "When I was neither a prophet nor the son of a prophet, but a herdsman and a treater of figs, Yahweh took me . . . and said, 'Go prophesy . . . . ' " Amos says in effect, I am a prophet; I take no orders from king or high priest, but they from me, and I from Yahweh. Such is the authority of Amos.

The imagery of "They shall wail the palace songs" is Amos-like. 8:3c is probably corrupt. 8:4–7 is a recomposition of 2:6–8 in the B editor's far more prosaic style, especially in the piling up of infinitives; nevertheless it preserves the lines of the oracle of Amos A well enough to be included unquestionably in the previous chapter.

As the calendar moves from late summer to early fall, from *qets* to *asip* according to the Gezer Calendar, the B editor makes allusion to the three major holy days that cluster at *succoth* (review Lev. 23:23–43). Amos 8:4–7 makes oblique reference to the first, the New Year, by adding the matter of the new moon to the critique as it appears in 2:6–7. The second holy day is the Day of Atonement, the unique day of repentance when Israel wards off the wrath of Yahweh. Recapitulating the motifs of lamentation and famine, and framed by references to the threatening day of Yahweh, 8:9–13 alludes to the mortification, mourning, and fasting of that solemn day. Its fasting is treated figuratively in continuity with the theme of the silencing of Amos, and with reference to Deut. 8:3. The entire section Amos 8:8–9:6 is framed by the metaphor of the rising and falling Nile. The turn of the year has reached its peak. Yahweh's rains are at hand. The altar at Bethel is crumbling to pieces. *Now* is the time to respond!

SUSPENDING THE DEATH SENTENCE

The components of the B stage not yet considered are the A-stage oracles contained therein largely unmodified, the oracles discussed in chapter 2. Now that God's death sentence is the issue in question rather than the result, how are these oracles to be read? What is their meaning in their new context? Some of these oracles are so explicit about Samaria that they can hardly be read in any but an historical sense, that is, as applying to Samaria and having been fulfilled. Their fulfillment serves as a warning that God follows through with his final sentence of death. But it's precisely the proof that God carries through that seems to preclude the other A-stage oracles, the ones that could apply to persons other than the ruling elite in Samaria, from making any sense in a context that leaves open the future for the readers' response. If an oracle says, "You shall die," how is it to be read in the B-stage context? One meaning is of course the one it, too, had for Samaria, the historical sense that is fulfilled. But can it contribute further to the meaning of a document whose weight is not in the past or future but the present?

Of course it can. Let me illustrate how by citing a short passage from near the end of Dickens's *A Christmas Carol.*

> "Spectre," said Scrooge, "something informs me that our parting moment is at hand. I know it, but I know not how. Tell me what man that was, with the covered face, whom we saw lying dead?"
>
> The Ghost of Christmas Yet To Come conveyed him to a dismal, wretched, ruinous churchyard.
>
> The Spirit stood among the graves, and pointed down to One.
>
> "Before I draw nearer to that stone to which you point, answer me one question. Are these the shadows of the things that Will be, or are they shadows of the things that May be only?"

Still the Ghost pointed downward to the grave by which it stood.

"Men's courses will foreshadow certain ends, to which, if persevered in, they must lead. But if the courses be departed from, the ends will change. Say it is thus with what you show me!"

The Spirit was immovable as ever.

Scrooge crept towards it, trembling as he went; and, following the finger, read upon the stone of the neglected grave his own name—EBENEZER SCROOGE.

"Am *I* that man who lay upon the bed? No, Spirit! O, no, no! Spirit! hear me! I am not the man I was. I will not be the man I must have been but for this intercourse. Why show me this, if I am past all hope? Assure me that I yet may change these shadows you have shown me by an altered life."

For the first time the kind hand faltered (*An Anthology of Famous British Stories*, New York: Random House, Inc., 1952, pp. 172–73).

Whatever contradiction there may be between the B stage and A stage arises out of the B editor's faith that God retains the initiative to judge. The B editor's faith corresponds, in other words, to God's plan in Ezekiel:

If I say to the wicked one, "You shall surely die," and he turns from his sin and performs right judgment and justice, he shall surely live; he shall not die (33:14–15).

The contradiction nevertheless creates a theological problem, a problem intensified in the C stage. What gives God the right to change his mind?

AUDIENCE, READERSHIP, SETTING, AND PURPOSE

"Seek not Bethel . . . set justice in the gate." The B editor ties the exhortation to justice to the opposition of Jerusalem to Bethel. *Justice and Jerusalem*—that is fundamental. The critical moment for making the commitment to justice bears down with full impact, and no further respite, at *succoth*, when the reader must respond to God's threatening appearance at the altar and, as it were, leave Bethel and go to

Jerusalem. The linkage of justice and Jerusalem amounts to the linkage of ethical responsibility with the maintenance of power. The integrity and ingenuousness of such a linkage are far from self-evident. It requires a closer look.

THE NORTHERNERS

The above summary suggests two distinct groups addressed by the B stage, northern Israelites and the Jerusalemite ruling elite. The first are the northerners. After the sack of Samaria, they continued to attend the rites at Bethel, which kept alive Yahwistic ceremonial, now stripped of the nationalistic implications it had during the northern monarchy. This northern group would have been composed largely, but not exclusively, of the peasantry. I want to call the northerners the *audience* of the B stage, to indicate that they were probably not the readers of Amos B, but only the hearers of a tradition, probably oral, that afterward became part of the written B-stage document. That tradition urged them to abandon Bethel in favor of Jerusalem as the place to celebrate their prosperity and identity. The tradition may go back to Amos A, but of that one cannot be sure.

There is clear evidence, however, that the tradition was in existence and functioning from the time of Hezekiah to the destruction of the altar of Bethel by Josiah. Chronicles reports, and there is no good reason to doubt it, that Hezekiah sent couriers to the north with an invitation to attend passover rites in Jerusalem (2 Chron. 30:1–12,18,25). Hezekiah named his son Manasseh after one of the chief tribes of the north, a move calculated to attract the allegiance of that region. He arranged for his son to marry a Galilean. The immigration of northerners to the south left its mark on both territories. In the north, Assyrian administrators were periodically forced, according to their own records and Ezra 4:2,9–10, to relocate peoples from other parts of their realm to the province of Samerina (the Assyrian name of north Israel after 721), due to the loss of peasantry to the south, despite what must have been at first a scarcity of land in Judah. In the south, recent archaeological study shows that Jerusalem first housed a major urban population at the end of the eighth century. At that time a wall was built to the west of Zion whose placement indicates that the population of Jerusalem expanded by as much as 200 percent within a few years. According to M. M. Eisman, "Parallel with the growth of Jerusalem, a number of sites in Judea show a similar but lesser expansion." The application of floodwater farming technology to the desert regions of eastern Judah during the seventh century led to the opening up of previously unproductive land, another indication of the influx of peasantry. Clearly Judah was able to appeal successfully to much of the northern population. Nevertheless, attracting them permanently away from the rites at Bethel, which lies so close to the border of the southern kingdom, took some persistence. Traditions like that defaming Bethel in Amos B played a significant role in Judah's prolonged appeal.

Eisman summarizes these developments as follows:

> The Davidic monarchy in Jerusalem was increasingly drawn to assert that Jerusalem was *the* center of the cult and that its Temple was *the* Temple of Yahweh. . . . [After 721] the position of the Jerusalemite monarchy was seen as vindicated by its survival in the face of the Assyrian threat. With large numbers of Israelites from the northern kingdom now in the south, and particularly in Jerusalem, the importance of the Temple was substantially increased. It had, in fact, ceased to be primarily a royal sanctuary and chapel. Now it had become the rallying center of the 'Mosaic' faith so clearly set out in Deuteronomy. Thus, these two factors—the joining together of peoples to create an urban Jerusalem and the emerging dominance of Deuteronomic monotheism through the reforms of Hezekiah and Josiah—are bound to one another. Such was the nature of the critical transformation that took place in 8th- and 7th-century Jerusalem (*Biblical Archaeologist* [1978], 41:53).

The centralization to which the Israelite peasantry, including those who were relatively well-off, gradually acceded had important socioeconomic consequences as well. Seal impressions that pinpoint the geographical extent of Jerusalem's control over wine production during the seventh century, for example, have been found only in Judah, with the exception of Gezer and Jericho, both very close to the border. Samerina obviously controlled the vintage of the north. The Judean rulers sought to shift this control as much as possible in their own direction, within the bounds allowed by the Assyrian administrators of the north, as long as they remained in power. The celebration of *succoth* in Jerusalem contributed greatly to that shift. This gives some idea of the reach for power whose noonday coincided with the reign of Josiah and whose propaganda precipitated into writing in the B stage of Amos.

THE JERUSALEMITE RULING ELITE

The second distinct group addressed by the B stage is the Jerusalemite ruling elite, beginning with the king. They hold positions in society wherein they can "love good" by concrete acts, by a commitment to justice that issues in just decisions. These addressees are policy makers, in possession of power and authority. They are in control. The basic moral premise that persons control their actions and can act to enhance or achieve justice in human relations, at least within the parameters fixed by the relatively inflexible processes of an agrarian society, applies to them more completely than to any other group in Judah. They enjoy a promising outlook. The B editor does what he can to portray their future as profoundly contingent, but for the present they live without the desperation to which the only response is a struggle or a cry and which would make the moral premise practically irrelevant to them.

The Jerusalemite ruling elite are the *readers* of the B stage: they have direct access to the B stage as a document, to read it or have it read to them. The polemic against pilgrimage to Bethel is not directed orally toward them, as though they had to choose between Bethel and Jerusalem, but is absorbed into the written document they read to provide, in conjunction with the destruction of the altar at Bethel, further validation for the authority of the B-stage work, for the unique role of Jerusalem as *the* cult center, and therefore for their status. Given the inherently problematic nature of the linkage of ethical responsibility with the maintenance of power, Amos B must strive for the highest degree of authority it can attain.

This device is identical to the validation of the Torah document, roughly Deuteronomy 12–28, by the first edition of the Deuteronomistic History, whose narrative proves the uniqueness of the house of Yahweh and the house of David in Jerusalem. Although the exact relationship of Amos B to the Deuteronomistic History is not known, the many ideological points of contact already mentioned are basic to both works. Pretending to ground power in justice, both documents in part ground justice in power. The starting point of both is the oneness of God's worship (based on the oneness of God) and therefore the uniqueness of Jerusalem, a deduction not at all self-evident prior to the period of Amos B. The political corollary of the oneness of God's worship is the oneness of God's people. Both works integrate premonarchic with monarchic, prophetic with monarchist, ideals. They preserve (which is to contain and institutionalize) prophetic tradition for two inherently competing purposes: (1) to justify the exclusive prerogatives of the Jerusalemite ruling elite and its cult, and (2) to hold the ruling elite accountable to their professed allegiance to the fundamentals of Yahwistic justice. The ideal synthesis highlighted by the Deuteronomist, Yahweh's raising of David from weakness to strength and setting him astride two social systems, the Mosaic and the monarchist, with their divergent sets of values, finds its analogue in Amos B's reference to the exodus (2:9–12) and in its exhortation to justice by the urban elite in terms of traditional village justice "in the gate." Amos B shares with the Deuteronomist the conviction that the decision for justice is critical but fragile. Both focus that decision on paradigmatic individuals, especially the king (Deut. 17:18–20; Amos 7:10–17). And they share a faith that institutions possessing power are capable, through their leaders, of acts of justice.

But power corrupts, and the powerful are the last to agree. The ingenuousness of the linkage of ethical responsibility with the maintenance of power is questionable not only by itself, but also because of the B editor's original connection to the ruling elite. In all likelihood Amos B was composed by a

Jerusalemite scribe, who like any other artisan specialist in an agrarian society performed at the beck and call of the ruling elite. The B editor could even have been a scribe belonging to the immediate court of Josiah or Jehoiakim. The conflict of interest inherent in this authorship seriously reduces the independence of the B editor from the group he so urgently addresses and suggests, to overstate the matter, that in Amos B the ruling elite is talking to itself, the equivalent in our society of institutional self-regulation. The very social group that Amos condemned in Samaria is now, in Jerusalem, sponsoring the preservation of his oracles.

Not much is known about this class of scribes, despite the fact that most of the Old Testament as presently composed is the product of their toil. We have already talked some about the values expressed and maintained through the literary intricacies of the B stage. Think of the long-range planning that went into executing such a composition, the leisure time it required, and who fed, clothed, and sheltered the author during his work. All these suggest the degree of patronage that attended the composition of Amos B. The scribe here functions not only as a bureaucratic recorder, but as a religious specialist who investigates, synthesizes, and seeks higher-order meanings in traditional peasant and peasant-related lore. In this office as well the scribe is largely subservient to the normal alliance of clergy and elite, the priesthood with the rulers. His work serves the needs primarily of these masters, not of the person or people from whom much of his raw material ultimately derives.

The scribe's essential function is to write. Why does he write? In an agrarian society writing is not nearly so widespread as it is in our society, but tends for all practical purposes to be limited to major urban centers and their rural bureaucratic outposts, and within these to a group of trained scribes, especially when it comes to longer works like Amos B. In an agrarian setting, writing is primarily a means of ownership definition, of social organization, and therefore of social control. Writing accomplishes this control because of its ability not only to create order but literally to *preserve order*. As a rule, order is preserved to the benefit of those who enjoy power and privilege within that order. To reorder the oracles of Amos and preserve their new order, with all the modified meanings that new order incorporates, represents one more procedure of social control available to and utilized by the ruling elite. Royal control of literary symbols is an extension of royal control of the symbols of the cult.

In the linkage of justice and Jerusalem, responsibility and the maintenance of power, reform and centralization, the scribe and the written document contribute by their nature and allegiance to the side of the tension that represents the maintenance of Jerusalemite power as well as to the side of reform. The cost for having the Jerusalemite monarchy sponsor the preservation of prophetic traditions that conceive of monarchy as a subordinate power is the validation of Jerusalem's power and perspective, from Jerusalem out (1:2). Given the social setting of writing in ancient Israel, the preservation of prophecy would seem unavoidably to require some such trade-off. Some kind of control of prophecy is practically the prerequisite of its preservation in this medium.

But that raises the question, Why preserve prophecy? Is it preserved for its own sake, or for the sake of the validation it confers upon some ulterior purpose? It is safe to say that the oracles of Amos would not have gotten through to future generations had they not been preserved in writing, but it would be wrong to infer that the claim for justice and the prophetic sense of and appeal for justice do not arise again and again with or without the writing down of prophecy. They would arise, but not among the ruling elite in such a way as to have a lasting effect on policy. The only way these can speak effectively to the ruling elite in their own setting is by speaking through a medium utilized by the elite. Writing is such a medium. I can imagine that, besides the B editor's faith that power-holders are capable of acts of justice, he also had a faith that writing could somehow work where speaking failed; a faith that the relative permanence and authority of his medium could be put to the service of God's and the prophet's authority as well as the king's; and a faith that the preservation of prophecy could mitigate injustice as permanently as writing is permanent. His faith may seem self-

serving for a scribe, even when it is remembered that he may
have been acting at the behest of the king himself. Without
denying this faith, we must still ask of both of them: given
their stake in the document, does their faith really go beyond the expression of mundane power through a mundane
medium?

To attempt to articulate the B editor's faith is thus not to
offer an apology for his work. The work's mundane aspects
are simply not to be gainsaid. The implicit claim to have
integrated ethical responsibility and the maintenance of
power without jeopardizing the former is a bold act of faith
that requires an extraordinary authority to substantiate it,
since it has so often in human experience proven to be a
delusion. The B editor compromises and depends on the
authority of *both* Amos and Jerusalem. His act of faith in
justice is ambiguous, as is every act of faith in justice in the
context of the maintenance of power.

Does the B editor's medium of writing, an elitist medium,
inevitably taint his ideals? If prophecy is institutionalized, is it
not inevitably tamed and domesticated? Is it not true that
justice is never given, but always exacted? Can a grasp for
power by the powerful at the same time be a stroke for justice? Is the B editor's faith naive? Has he been used? I ask this
insistent battery of questions not to deny the truth and effec-
tiveness of the B editor's faith, but to spotlight its problematic
character. The linkage of responsibility with the maintenance
of power is *always* problematic. There may be no alternative
way to institutionalize justice. There may be no genuine alternative way to bring prophecy effectively to bear on power
but to institutionalize it, in writing as in other ways, and call
it prophecy grown up, or justice in the process of being
achieved in the midst of the ambiguities of human affairs.
But to fail to question the linkage of responsibility and the
maintenance of power, to fail to be alert to its problematic
character, is the surest way to condone the institutionalization
of injustice.

The B stage, then, was composed in Jerusalem late in
the seventh century by a scribal adjunct to the ruling elite;
through writing and the art of literature, he expresses and

preserves on behalf of the ruling elite the desire to maintain the status and power of Jerusalem as a sociopolitical center, and the motivation to put this power to use in a program of customary and judicial reform. The medium of the B stage is likewise inherently problematic. Literature is analogous to an institution, and the containment of prophecy in literature to the containment of prophetic consciousness in government or the church. They serve the same purposes and carry the same risks. Prophetic consciousness might not reach the elite unless it is institutionalized. But does it become tame when controlled by the orderly, and powerless when contained by the powerful? The Bible itself embodies this risk. We easily forget how often in the history of Christianity it has functioned as a means of political power because at present its realm of influence is so shrunken. Christians have always had to struggle to use the Bible not for the maintenance of power that controls but rather for the attainment of power that liberates. The B stage of the book of Amos stands as a statement of faith that, perilous, pretentious, and futile though their attempt could be, nevertheless the elite must try to appropriate the prophetic voice not to consolidate their own controlling power but to tap its liberating power.

PRELITERARY SETTING OF B-STAGE MATERIAL

The B-stage editor did not invent the polemic against Bethel or the exhortation to justice. His document represents the literary deposit of many concerns and statements coming from places other than Jerusalem, going back long before the seventh century, and not necessarily implying at all the same things they came to imply in the B-stage document. In order to avoid the merest suspicion that such material pertains exclusively to seventh-century Jerusalem, I want to describe its preliterary settings and meanings with some thoroughness.

Prophets like Amos, and perhaps Amos himself, were deeply committed, like the B editor, to the critique of the pilgrimage rites at Bethel, Dan, Gilgal, Beersheba, and other sanctuaries—if with different premises from those of the B editor. Prophets like Amos, and perhaps Amos himself, exhorted to justice, warned of the consequences of failing to decide justly, and, needless to say, bore the scornful and shortsighted response. Looked at in *this* way, the significant differences between the A and B stages are not the chronological and geographical ones, but those which depend on the wider audience and more traditional social setting of the pilgrimage festival. In other words, the distinctive literary features of the A and B stages differ not only because the B stage was composed a hundred years after Amos in another part of the land, but also, from the preliterary perspective, because they emerge out of two different polemical contexts. One is directed at the exclusive ruling elite in Samaria, and the other is addressed to the inclusive population in attendance at Bethel.

Whether Amos himself was the preliterary source of the B materials, or of some of them, in this sense is moot. The ambiguity is like the ambiguity as to whether the narrative in 7:1–9:6 goes back in some way to Amos. To say B-stage materials go back to Amos in their preliterary form would provide a satisfying and needful solution to the problem of why the different prophetic collections are as distinctive from one another as they are. There is, however, an interesting bit of evidence that forces me to leave this question unsettled. If my analysis of the A stage is correct, Amos mentions *succoth*:

> I will turn your pilgrimage feasts into mourning
> And all your songs into lamentation (8:10).

With this statement we should probably include the fragment in 8:3: "They shall wail the palace songs." The B stage seems to me to say something quite different about the same thing:

> I hate, I spurn your pilgrimage feasts . . .
> Remove from me the commotion of your songs
> The playing of your harps let me not attend (5:21,23).

In the A stage, Yahweh holds the initiative: *he* will transform songs of joy into wailings for the dead, the ruling elite. In the B stage, the people, *you*, hold the initiative: put aside your songs and take up the task of justice. Do these two views about the same thing differ because they belong to different polemical contexts or because one goes back to Amos and the other does not? The presence of the ruling elite in the audience of both contexts perpetuates, it seems to me, the ambiguity, at least in the case of the pilgrimage feast.

In other cases, the literary analysis of the B stage only defines the B-stage meaning of a phrase or line that goes back to the A stage and probably Amos. A case in point is the combination of "winter house" and "summer house" in 3:15. Although not strictly speaking in parallelism, these phrases, when translated this way, could represent a parallel pair culled from a poetic oracle of Amos. They refer to a specific feature of the social cleavage that obsessed Amos. It is common in agrarian societies for members of the ruling elite to move from residence to residence for their comfort as the seasons require. In the most recent critical treatment of these phrases, Shalom Paul concludes, "The wealthy residents of Samaria followed the example of royalty and built for themselves separate pleasure estates in accordance with the climatic conditions of their country" (*Vetus Testamentum* 28 [1978] 358–60).

The same relative certainty applies to parts of the B stage that most likely do *not* go back to Amos. The descriptions of Yahweh that serve the purpose of theophanies are an example (4:13; 5:8; 9:5–6). Except for some phrases that relate more directly to the literary B stage, these doxologies catalogue the attributes of Yahweh that empower him regularly to cause the fall rains. The elaboration of the theological basis of the regularity of the rains could almost be said to be at the polar opposite from Amos's style and subject, and to lack any prophetic component whatsoever until placed in a context, the B stage, which makes the cosmic change of seasons contingent. The doxologies probably derive, little changed, from liturgical prescriptions for *succoth,* whether celebrated in Bethel, Jerusalem, or elsewhere.

The same derivation is indicated for much of the material whose ultimate source is ambiguous: the traditions of exhortation and warning, and particularly those oracles that belong to the type of speech called litigation, or "covenant lawsuit (*rib*)." Amos 5:21–24 shares significant features with a type of oracle of which at least one example appears in nearly every prophetic collection. The tendency—supported, paradoxically, by this very type of oracle—is to set prophet over against cult and to associate the exhortation to justice embodied in the litigation form with the prophetic side of the opposition. This form is widely held by scholars, however, to have its original setting in ritual. Although there is, predictably, disagreement as to exactly what kind of ritual, any of the options currently being considered could be a part of the ceremonial of *succoth*. To set prophet against cult in any simple way is to forget that the traditions of justice—story, contract, stipulations, sanctions—that we call prophetic provided a major portion of the tradition celebrated in the pilgrimage feasts and that the commandment to keep these feasts is included in all the major covenant law codes. The audience at Bethel knew, faintly at least, what right judgment and justice were. Whatever vagueness attaches to these traditions is explainable in terms of not only the mixed constituency of the rites, but also the need to state the positive ideal of justice in a way that allowed for the complexities of societal relationships. The rites contained within themselves the means of their own critique. The issue at stake, therefore, is not that Amos 5:21–24 might or might not simply go back to Amos, but that, whether it was Amos who adapted it or someone else, it goes back, as it were, even further: it exemplifies a type whose form is intimately tied to the festival rites of Bethel.

To describe the critique of the pilgrimage feast in terms of the same view of society and the same conception of justice that pertained to the A stage is to draw tight the line that connects the preliterary stage of the B document with Amos. The critique is not necessarily Amos's, but it is a necessary corollary of Amos's view of society and theological convictions.

I want to describe this critique in terms of five points. First, the conspicuous consumption of the pilgrimage feast, particularly as it draws most heavily on the vintage, represents the same ease and enjoyment, the carelessness, of the feasting of the elite in Samaria. The B editor himself makes this equation by adding "in the house of their god" (for the B editor, the shrine of Bethel) to "they drink the wine of those they mulct" in 2:8b. But whether it was at the expense of the poor or to their benefit, for they were there, is ambiguous. The prophetic critique raises the question, What constitutes the service of God? The sacrifices held during the pilgrimage feast were consumed by the congregation, including presumably the needy, or, in the case of the holocausts, by no one. That is all right when otherwise all segments of society are being fed adequately. But when hunger is common, the price in food and in the waste that such sacrifice can symbolize is too great for the ideological return, itself of questionable value. When hunger is common, the better service of God is not the display of the ideology of justice, but its realization. The critique is not of the comfortable pew per se—God wants his people to sit in comfortable pews—but of the symbolic expression of an imbalance in priorities as long as what the pews stand for is for the few.

The second point is equally obvious, yet never seems to become dispensable. Worship in fixed forms tends *in part* to be felt and practiced as the automatic propitiation of God. This liability of worship is the other side of its strength, the strength of habit, but it can be as habitual as sin. The critique of the Bethel rites in its preliterary stage exposes the game of "Schlemiel" described by Eric Berne in his book *Games People Play*: a person goes through the week hurting people, repeats a formulaic "I'm sorry" (the words are an escape and vague enough to cover a multitude of sins) on Sunday, and leaves church with an "assurance"—the word says it all—of pardon, to start the same week all over again. The critique condemns the corrupt economy of the well-to-do's clean conscience.

The third point has to do with the tithe. "Present . . . your tithes on the third day" (4:4). The festival gatherings at Bethel were provided in large measure by the tithe. The tithe was a 10 percent tax on produce, probably conceived of as a land tax on Yahweh's land, administered by the religious elite. In deuteronomistic ideology, which in this matter no doubt comes close to representing premonarchic thinking, the presentation of the tithe serves to reinforce the attitude that the cultivation of Yahweh's land is contingent, that the people can use their lands only so long as they adhere to Yahweh's stipulations for a just society. Every third year, according to Deut. 14:22–29, the tithe was to be distributed to the poor. But once again what began as egalitarian ideology can end up as corrupt economics. If as a member of the elite much of your land does not fall in the category of redistributional lands, your sense of Yahweh's ownership of your land must, no matter what rites reinforce it, be greatly attenuated. As for the peasantry, as soon as they are reduced to bare subsistence, any contribution to the community's ceremonial fund is a heavy, potentially unbearable burden for them. In and of itself, furthermore, the tithe works to the advantage of the prosperous: any straight percentage tax is by nature regressive.

"Do not prophesy at Bethel anymore, for it is the sanctuary of the king, the temple of the kingdom." The bringing of sacred offerings to God at Bethel was analogous to the secular provisioning of the royal household in Samaria (as in 1 Kings 4–5, the provisioning of Solomon's court). The royal elite in Israel had a strong influence on, and probably control over, the religious elite at Bethel (Amos 7:10,13). What was supposed to be Yahweh's shrine threatened to become the king's shrine, as Amaziah says. The fourth point is therefore this: insofar as royalty encouraged and condoned the oppression of the peasantry, and virulent rent capitalism originated in royal policy, the sacred ceremonial in effect imitated and became a sanction for the exploitation of the poor. Under such circumstances worship becomes one more weapon in the elite's arsenal, by which the term *justice* and its ideological representation subtly legitimate a system of injustice. This insidious development can occur wherever the religious establishment is under the strong influence of the powerful in society and their values and so sanctions, directly or tacitly, an oppressive societal status quo.

And fifth, the peasantry willingly participated, to the prophet's dismay. Those who condone and defend the class system, especially in an agrarian society, have never consisted of just the members of the ruling elite. The system could not function if that were the case. The sanctuary, its ceremonial, and the social schema and values it represented made an enormous impact on the peasantry's sense of purpose, place, and identity. They seized on this apparent boon gladly, particularly those who were upwardly mobile, taking advantage of economic distress to increase their wealth and possibly move up in class. Administering this ceremonial was the function of the ruling elite. Thus the king had the power to reinforce the peasant's sense of identity in terms of the very royalty that was oppressing him, and the priest had the power to reinforce his spiritual identity in terms of the very service of God that legitimated his oppression. This is the religious version of an old story: the more powerful have the less powerful coming and going.

You may have found that when I said "ritual" or the like, you thought of "them," and when I said "worship," you thought of yourself as well. What role, we might well ask ourselves, does worship play in our churches, and in our society, really? It is easy to become simplistically moralistic on this subject—a temptation to be avoided if only because it trivializes and thus discredits valid moral critique. But that does not excuse us from looking clear-sightedly at the functioning of worship in our own society.

4

Exile and Beyond:
Stage C

No one ever learns from anyone else's mistakes; everyone has to make his or her own. If the B editor had believed that, he might never have composed his work. But seventy-five years later it seemed very true indeed. The ruling elite of Jerusalem had failed the test set by the B stage and as a consequence—so it could be believed among the elite—suffered the same punishment as the ruling elite in Samaria. They had gone into exile to die.

Almost all of them, that is. Some survived. More exactly, isolated groups and individuals from the second and third generations of the elite who went into exile remembered enough and preserved among themselves enough of the old writings to retain their identity as Yahweh's people, despite their punishment. Or perhaps because of it: looked at theologically, their exile served as one more proof of God's justice and God's protection of the powerless. Now that *they* were the relatively powerless—a crucial point—God's justice was for once a source of strength they could, from their point of view, justly claim as their due. From these seeds a new community would grow. This in essence was the message of Second Isaiah and of other exilic editions of prophetic collections. And this is the message of the C stage of the book of Amos, the book taken in its entirety.

A resourceful, imaginative scribe who picked up and read the B stage of Amos sometime in the last third of the sixth century B.C. would have had the overpowering impression that some major changes had taken place since the days of Josiah and Jehoiakim, when the B stage was written. Not only did B's challenge of just rule fail decisively to gain a hearing a generation or two back, but also, as for the present, it was not at all clear what role if any the elite in exile who retained their Yahwistic identity would play in a new government in Israel under Persian hegemony. It was not the challenge to do justice that spoke most directly to this new generation, but the challenge to claim justice on their own behalf and to have faith that Yahweh would rescue the relatively powerless from death and restore them to life as he had in the past.

On the other side of the watershed of the Babylonian exile, in the transition from independent kingdom to province of the Persian Empire, the old archival documents, among them the B stage of Amos, had to be updated. For Amos this updating involved two major changes: (1) the *beginning* of the B document was recomposed with the addition of 1:9–12 and 2:4–5, and (2) the *end* of the B document was extended by the addition of 9:7–15. There were a few other minor changes in the main body of the work ("Zion" in 6:1 is a candidate), and its eventual juxtaposition with Joel may have produced some slight changes in the way it was read. You might think that changes like these would make little overall difference in the book, and from a modern perspective you would probably be right. According to the literary conventions that applied to ancient biblical literature, however, the beginning and end of a work were its most important parts. Thus to its original readers, Amos C is, by virtue of its new beginning and end, an entirely new work, even though the B stage within it remains for the most part intact. For some time I called this new beginning and end its prelude and postlude. But I have given up these designations because they imply that the beginning and end are somehow extra rather than indispensable. Without its new exoskeleton, the work would have disintegrated in its new environment for lack of interested readers.

It is useful to look at the C stage in terms of *reversal*. If the exile represented the A stage fulfilled a second time, the C stage represents the A stage standing on its head. Look at these examples of explicit reversal.

> The virgin Israel has fallen down—
> No more to rise
> She is left abandoned on the ground—
> No one to raise her (5:2).
> They have fallen and shall not rise again (8:14).
> I shall raise the fallen hut of David (9:11).

* * *

> The delightful vineyards you have planted—
> You shall not drink their wine (5:11).
> They shall plant vineyards and drink their wine (9:14).

* * *

> I shall not cause him to return (2:4).
> I shall return the captivity of my people (9:14).

The C stage cannot simply assert these contradictions. It must also offer some kind of explanation as to why the conclusion should be right—not necessarily a reason to satisfy a logical mind, but at least a way of conceiving of this new message *in relation to* the previous message. It does this in two ways. The beginning deals with the reversal in terms of God's standards of justice, the end in terms of the experience of the festival of *succoth* and what that conveys about the people's relationship to God. In other words, far from skirting the main issues of its base document, the C stage accepts their value, adopts them, and presses them to apply with equal integrity to a new age.

THE BEGINNING: GOD'S UNMOLLIFIED WRATH IS UNJUST

The oracles against Tyre, Edom, and Judah bracketed in chapter 3 were composed and added by the C editor.

> Thus says Yahweh:
> For three transgressions of Tyre and for four
> I shall not cause it to return—
> Because they delivered Edom into a total exile
> And did not remember the covenant of brothers (1:9).

> Thus says Yahweh:
> For three transgressions of Edom and for four
> I shall not cause it to return—

Because he pursued his brother with the sword
  And repudiated his covenant mercy
And his anger raged forever
  And his wrath was wild always (1:11).

Thus says Yahweh:
For three transgressions of Judah and for four
I shall not cause it to return—
Because they rejected the instruction of Yahweh
  And his statutes they did not keep
And their "lies" which their fathers walked after led
  them astray (2:4).

The C editor seems to have imitated the B-stage model, or the common source they both shared for these oracles, and modified them slightly from the model in order to make them stand out for the elite readers who were attuned to such subtleties. The oracle against Judah is an obvious choice for updating the set to take into account the Babylonian exile. Its language is prosaic, extremely general, and emphasizes idolatry, like the second, or exilic, edition of the Deuteronomistic History (Dtr 2). For the C editor, insofar as Judah takes Israel's place as the culminating oracle, the earlier group of "example" nations is reorganized to center Tyre and Edom:

$$\left\{ \begin{array}{l} \text{Aram} \\ \text{Philistia} \end{array} \right.$$

Tyre
Edom

$$\left\{ \begin{array}{l} \text{Ammonites} \\ \text{Moab} \end{array} \right.$$

Judah

Tyre and Edom are probably grouped together in this stage because in the immediate postexilic period they represented Judah's most vehement mercantile competitors. On the other hand, insofar as "Israel," now represented by the people of Judah, keeps the place it had in the B stage as the culminating oracle, Edom is centered in the group of seven examples:

$\left\{\begin{array}{l}\text{Aram}\\ \text{Philistia}\\ \text{Tyre}\end{array}\right.$

Edom

$\left\{\begin{array}{l}\text{Ammonites}\\ \text{Moab}\\ \text{Judah}\end{array}\right.$

"Israel"

Edom is singled out for peculiar animosity in several passages dating to this period: Ps. 137:7; Joel 3:19; Isa. 63:1–6; Mal. 1:2–4; Obadiah; and especially Amos 9:12, which sets Judah and Edom in opposition. Any way it is considered, the oracles against the nations are organized in the C stage to echo late exilic and postexilic concerns.

A pattern emerges in the C set of oracles that potentially has an unresolved outcome. We'll put the transgressors of the C-stage oracles in the left column and their victims in the right.

Transgressor	Wronged One
Tyre	Edom
Edom	brother (Judah is what's left of Israel)
Judah	Yahweh
Yahweh?	his people?

At each succeeding step, the wronged one regularly turns out to be the wrong one. Could that include Yahweh?

Tyre's transgression is to "deliver Edom into a *total exile*." What that means is implied by the measure-for-measure punishment pronounced against Philistia for the same transgression: "the remnant of the Philistines will perish," i.e., there will be *no one left*. Edom's transgression is to repudiate the notion of mercy, allow his anger to burn ceaselessly, and so disregard the traditional expectation that one covenant partner might give another the benefit of mercy and forgive him his covenant transgressions. In other words, as the *exile* imposed by Tyre was *total*, so the *wrath* nursed by Edom was *total*. These are the arch-unforgivable transgressions according to the C editor: total exile and total wrath.

Unforgivable? That seems to be the categorical meaning of the expression "I shall not cause it to return" repeated eight times in these oracles. But what is the "it" in this expression? The common view is that "it" refers to Yahweh's judgment, the word of punishment that follows in each case. Thus the RSV translates, "I shall not revoke the punishment," which is not wrong, just not precise enough. The difficulty with this and several other suggested translations is that they do not have in mind a specific antecedent for "it," and parallels indicate one is needed. There are two probable antecedents, "people (*am*)" and "anger (*ap*)." The ambiguous pronoun "it" is used in order to allow the line to refer to both of these antecedents at once.

With the first antecedent, "people," the meaning of the expression is, "I shall not cause the people to return (from exile)." This meaning applies directly to oracles in which the transgressor is explicitly condemned to exile: Aram ("the people of Aram shall go into exile to Qir"), Philistia ("the remnant of Philistia shall perish"), and the Ammonites ("their king shall go into exile"). It applies indirectly to the rest of the oracles where, for the C stage's readers, exile implicitly follows destruction, as everyone knows it does in 2:6–16.

With the second antecedent, "anger," the meaning of the expression is, "I shall not cause (my) anger to return." This is part of a common idiom that pictures someone "sending" anger and "causing it to return" as an expression of wrath and its mollification. Thus "I shall not cause it to return" means "I shall not be mollified." Ps. 78:38 provides a good example of its use:

> But he was merciful
>> He forgave their iniquity
>> He did not repudiate (mercy)
>> And he plenteously caused his anger to return
>> And did not stir up all his wrath.

Ps. 78 and other contexts where this idiom occurs show that it usually involves a concern with the quantity of God's patience, the degree of his mercy, and the extent of what he will tolerate in order to relent. This is especially clear in the refrain in Isa. 5:25; 9:12,17,21; 10:4:

> For all this his anger has not (yet) returned
> And his hand is stretched out still.

What Yahweh says over and over, therefore, in the beginning of the book of Amos, is: For their transgressions I shall deliver them into exile and destroy every remnant (total exile), and I shall never be mollified (total wrath).

But those are precisely the transgressions of Tyre and Edom! Yahweh has condemned the punishments of total exile and total wrath. To inflict them is transgression. The paradox is that he is culpable of the same transgressions. Or so it seems to be suggested. Perhaps Yahweh does belong at the bottom of the "Transgressor" column. Certainly the question is raised, Will Yahweh hold himself to his own standards of just mercy?

It is raised, at any rate, if one studies the details of this first section of C as we have just done. I dare say the problem has not jumped out at you before. But then we do not usually read the book of Amos the way the C editor meant it to be read—in Hebrew, paying close attention to structural detail, and taking it as an integrated whole. If it is read as an integrated whole, you cannot read the end without having to think back again to the beginning and ask, in effect, how did we get from there to here? Perhaps only then do you notice that, with the oracles against Tyre and Edom, Yahweh has painted himself into a corner.

I am reminded of the original film version of *The Wizard of Oz*. The beginning of the film shows a bit of Kansas farm life at Dorothy's house. When Judy Garland as Dorothy fell into the pigpen, farmhand Bert Lahr (who later is seen as the lion) jumped in and saved her, and Jack Haley (later the tin woodsman) nearly burst into tears when he found out about it. When Miss Gulch, the angry neighbor, threatened to take Toto the dog away, farmhand Ray Bolger (appearing later as the scarecrow) made an intelligent response that silenced the old maid. Now these three, you'll remember—the lion, the tin man, and the scarecrow—were supposed to lack, respectively, courage, heart, and brain. When at the end of the film the Wizard gives them each what he lacks, you think back and recall that, yes, they did possess these qualities all along. In fact—and this you realize only at the end—that's the significance, in the context of the whole film, of the particular incidents shown in the beginning. In other words, those initial incidents were addressing an issue that hadn't been clearly raised yet.

With this comparison—or any murder mystery, for that matter—in mind, the literary technique of the C-stage editor no longer seems remarkable at all. Don't forget, however, that reading Amos C in Hebrew, even in sixth-century B.C. Babylon or Jerusalem, and watching *The Wizard of Oz* on the screen are two entirely different affairs. The one requires years of training and membership in a relatively exclusive guild; the other is as widely accessible, or so I've supposed in referring to it, as vanilla ice cream. The intellectual and literary consideration of justice is not for everyone, but it is for some. We have already seen that a society might be potentially better for it. The society of late sixth-century Judah, to the degree that it depended on the recovery or formation of an identity among its elite, wouldn't have existed without it.

THE END: GOD'S MERCY IS JUST

Yahweh does adhere to his own standards of justice. The C editor waits till the end of his work to say so, but when he does, it is in a way that refers directly back to the beginning of the document where the issue is first hinted at.

> Are you not like the Cushites to me, O Israelites?—oracle of Yahweh. Did I not bring Israel up from the land of Egypt, the Philistines from Caphtor, and Aram from Qir (9:7)?

To paraphrase, Yahweh returns distant remnants from exile and mollifies his wrath. The categorical "I shall not cause it to return" turns out to be reversible.

The "children of the Cushites" have been taken to exemplify people on the periphery of the world, as seen from Jerusalem out, and thus people who come under God's aegis no matter how far they are from the homeland. I think the comparison is more specific than that. Since the Cushites are the first thing the C editor mentions when his voice resumes in his ending, he must have had a reason for choosing precisely these people for his example. The J tradition in Gen. 10:8–11, which the C editor could read in its present form, indicates his reason:

> Cush bore Nimrod . . . and the foremost (cities) of his [Nimrod's] kingdom were *Babylon*, Erek, Akkad, and *Kalneh*, in Mesopotamia. From that land he went out to *Assyria* and built Nineveh . . . .

The "children of the Cushites" in Amos 9:7 are not the Ethiopians but the Mesopotamians, Babylon and Assyria. The C editor's opening query therefore asks, "To me, are you not as good as the Assyrians and Babylonians who have afflicted you?" The implied answer is yes.

This reference to Genesis 10 clears up an apparent textual problem in the A-stage oracle in 6:2 as well. In chapter 2 I changed the text slightly to restore what I, and many other interpreters, conjecture were Amos's original words:

> Pass by Kullani and see
>> From there go to Hamath the great
>> Then go down to Gath of the Philistines
> Are you better than these kingdoms?
>> Is your territory greater than their territory?

Actually, the text says:

> Pass by *Kalneh* and see
>> From there go to Hamath the great [an *Aramean* city-
>> state]
>> Then go down to Gath of the *Philistines*
> Are there better than these kingdoms?
>> But is their territory greater than your territory?

Some interpreters choose to take these lines as they stand as a derisive quote by Amos of the elite assuring one another of their invulnerability. These interpreters could be right. But the similarity of the argument of the last two lines ("Are you not as good as these kingdoms?") to the argument of 9:7a suggests the C-stage editor recomposed them. He changed Kullani to Kalneh to turn the cities listed here into equivalents of the states referred to in 9:7.

> Kalneh:Cush
> Hamath:Aram
> Gath:Philistines

The C-stage editor's intent is to plant another clue to the end of the book of Amos in its midst.

What with his attention to the exact *words*, more than to the historical meaning, of the base texts he uses for composing 9:7 (Gen. 10:8–11, Amos 1:3–8, and Amos 6:2), it is fair to describe the C editor's technique as an early form of midrash, a more prevalent technique in the prophetic collections in their later stages of composition than is generally recognized. The C-stage editor represents the B-stage editor's scribalism compounded by the existence of a new assemblage of Yahwistic documents fast acquiring a primitive canonicity.

The exodus from Egypt is the most popular metaphor for the return from exile in the exilic period. Here it picks up the reference to the exodus in 2:9–10, with its allusion to the planting of Israel the vine, to foreshadow the imagery of the vineyard in 9:11–15 ("I shall plant them on their ground . . . " [9:15]). The oracle against Philistia in Jeremiah 47 designates the Philistines as "the remnant of the distant shore of Caphtor" (47:4). The historical significance of this designation is debated, but its literary significance in the C editor's mind is clear: it makes "Have I not brought the Philistines up from Caphtor" (I have saved the remnant of Caphtor) the reverse of "the remnant of the Philistines shall perish" (1:8). Finally, it goes without saying that "Have I not brought Aram up from Qir" reverses "the people of Aram shall go into exile to Qir" (1:5). (I have experimented with the possibility that the last phrase and 1:8b were modified or inserted by the C editor to prepare for 9:7. You might find it interesting to consider the pros and cons.) The order Philistia–Aram in 9:7 chiastically reverses the order Aram–Philistia in 1:3–8. Once again form mirrors content.

The pivotal keynote of the C stage is 9:7. Its rhetorical position is analogous to the phrase "Yahweh is his name" in 5:8 for the B stage. It resolves—or better, annuls—the two hard, paradoxical questions that automatically arise if the book of Amos is to continue to be meaningful to the restored community: Can total destruction possibly be just? Can restoration possibly be just? From here on the C editor is free to elaborate positively on Yahweh's restoration of Israel.

He does so in two steps. The first is in 9:8–10, a prose statement composed by the C editor to the effect that God will destroy a kingdom but not a people, and will make a separation of the sinful from the unsinful. The second step is in 9:11–15, a mostly poetic oracle adapted by the C editor to portray the restoration as a reconstruction and replanting of a vineyard. The first step is to make up a remnant, the second to restore it.

The basis for God's selection of the remnant is again his justice. Thus he excludes the "sinful" of his people. But just as the C editor probes the justice inherent in mercy indirectly, so he declines to define sinfulness in any straightforward manner. The book of Amos already includes God's condemnation of unjust behavior specifically defined (A stage) and God's exhortation to just behavior generally defined (B stage). From the C-stage point of view these are penultimate approaches to justice. They need completion. Having already said, through the inclusion of the A and B stages, if you do wrong you will die and I urge you to do right, the C editor looks to the future and pursues the matter a step further, asking, Who will hear the message? Who *will* obey God's stipulations? As the world shakes, the exiles wander aimlessly without satisfaction (the pebble "wanders" like the people in 4:8 and 8:12), homeless and persecuted. As they wander, God listens to them and hears two kinds of people. There are those who say, "The evil will not get to us," and by implication there are those who say "The evil has gotten to us." The former are unsuited for the new community. The latter make up the remnant.

For the C editor and his readers, the world of meaningful action lies in the future, not the past or present. With a view to the future, God judges attitude, not action. God is looking for what people today might call "readiness for justice." The people who say "The evil does not or will not get to us" are manifestly oblivious to God's attempts to get through to them, to those signs in the world and in their own experience that reveal God's justice. God's justice is hard enough to recognize under normal circumstances. To miss the point while tumbling rootless in a topsy-turvy world, with Amos B ringing in the ears to boot, is a sure indication that a person is ethically senseless. Such persons do not perceive or cannot believe they are vulnerable to God's justice; therefore, they are under no constraint to act justly. The reading of the curses of the covenant would only fall on their deaf ears. They would never *hear* (remember Dickie from chapter 2). Such persons are not ready, or fit, for the restored community of justice. This is not a new prophetic idea, but an updating and restatement of stage A (compare Jer. 5:12–14; Mic. 3:11).

After the elimination of the unfit, the second step is to restore the fit. What will their new, just community be like? At the end of the sixth century, the notion of a restored "kingdom" was strategically complicated, politically ambiguous, theologically problematic, and, as the next few years proved, it had an unlikely future. Instead of a kingdom, God reconstructs a vineyard.

> On that day
> I shall raise the fallen hut of David
>   And wall up their breaches
>   And raise its ruined walls
>   And so build it as in days of old
> (So that they can dispossess the remnant of Edom and of
>   all the nations against whom my name was called [in
>   1:3–2:3]—oracle of Yahweh, the one about to do this).
> The days are coming—oracle of Yahweh—when

The plowman will come together with the reaper
  And the treader of grapes with the sower of seed
And the mountains shall drip sweet wine
  And all the hills shall melt with it
And I shall return the captivity of my people Israel
  And they shall rebuild the desolated cities and dwell in
    them
And plant vineyards and drink their wine
  And make orchards and eat their fruit
And when I plant them on their land, they shall never
  again be pulled up from their ground, which I have
  given them—says Yahweh your God.

To many readers of Amos, if they are not sighing with relief at the good news, this oracle comes as something of a deflation. I used to wonder how, if I really took the rest of Amos seriously, I could possibly take this ending seriously. It's as though Amos, whose presence has been so powerful and self-assured up to this point, suddenly lapses into self-doubt and, distracted by the bromide that a negative is seldom satisfying, embarrassingly trips as he leaves the stage. We read it with a mildly cynical "Oh, yeah" in reaction to its sanguine disregard of what has gone before. Can this be prophecy?

A counterquestion: Where do you suppose the C editor got all that good poetry? He has already exposed his own stylistic hand in 9:7–10, and in 9:12 he inserts another line in prose about dispossessing Edom "and all the nations," a politically grandiose aside that shows his large faith but comes close to betraying the original intent of the poetic oracle—an intent I nevertheless think he understood. By now you know why we can skip a discussion of whether this oracle goes back to Amos. It's an unanswerable question. What we can say is that this oracle, like Isa. 9:2–7, 11:1–9, Mic. 4:1–4, 5:2–4, and similar passages, represents the other side of the coin of prophecies of doom: in place of the society that is destroyed another society must be built, and the earlier prophets were concerned with the new society as well as the old.

The visions of reconstruction that go back to the prophets who lived during the monarchy tend to emphasize the thoroughgoing recovery of justice. This justice is usually embodied in transformed monarchist figures, as in the examples from Isaiah and Micah, but sometimes these monarchist figures are minimized, as in Amos 9:11–15. Restoration requires restructuring the entire society. This oracle is no Annie Oakley to Brook Farm. It is a disruptive vision of a whole society that can preserve justice without an imperialist monarch (despite the C editor's scheme in 9:12), a royal temple, a capital city, or a centralized government. (Whether it can do without prophetic scribes like the C editor, or without writing, for that matter, isn't broached.) Its imagery reverts to Israel's earliest traditions, reaching back to the premonarchic period and to David before he came to Jerusalem, when the heroes of the people fought for their liberation against the monarchist institutions of the land. In its oral stage this oracle was addressed to the oppressed segments of society, the peasantry. It does not refer to the peasantry as a remnant, any more than Amos ever did. "Remnant" implies minority, even in Hebrew, and would never suit the peasantry, who made up 80 percent or more of the population. "Remnant" is used by B- and C-type editors to refer to the leftover ruling elite.

In the C editor's mind, the millennial dream involves the whole population, both the remnant of the elite who have returned and the other components of the population in the land. When the remnant return they join a restored society of a type not seen since the early days of David and before, or so it was thought. To be a part would require a commitment and faith quite without parallel in a world structured for "more of the same." The remnant are in for some occupational retooling. The C editor's faith in God's new vineyard is optimistic, though not cheery, and too whole to be naive.

The new exodus is like the first exodus, a liberation from servitude to and oppressive exploitation by the ruling elite. The new community returns again to the land, or better, the land returns to the new community. The peasantry recover their domain. The vineyards, orchards, and grain lands become theirs again, and they are the ones who reside comfortably in the cities, not their oppressors.

123

The hut, or booth (*succah*), of David is an intriguing image. It never ceases to attract the attention of interpreters because it has no obvious referent—nowhere else is a booth of David mentioned—and because, as the sole hint of a monarchist aspect to this vision, it must bear a lot of weight if the entire oracle is taken to allude to the rebuilding of the temple or the restoration of the kingdom. We have already seen, however, that the monarchist sympathies of the C editor are lukewarm at best, and those of the original oracle decidedly cool.

Obviously the image of David's hut is determinative, standing as it does at the beginning of the oracle. There's no reason why an image that holds such an important position should be obscure. In fact, it's not. The hut was a temporary structure constructed in the vineyard to shelter workers during the preparation of its wall and ground, the vine work, and the vintage. It served as well as the focal point of the local festivities that accompanied the making of new wine. The other distinctive terms in the first four lines of this oracle, "wall," "breach," "ruin," and "build," can refer, in combination with "hut," to only one possible setting—the vineyard. The "hut" was a gazebo: it had no walls, only a leafy roof supported by posts at four corners. The ruined walls that are being put back together here are not its walls, but the stone walls Yahweh tore apart when he destroyed his vineyard Israel, as in Isa. 5:1–7. The hut, then, is simply the first structure that goes up as the workman sets about to repair the vineyard. The first thing the gardner does is to get ready for his siesta.

But why, if the oracle is intended to portray an alternative to monarchist institutions, does it mention David? The reference is to the early David, the folk hero, the protector of the disenfranchised, the David of the byways and caves of the Judean hill country, sprung from the country town of Bethlehem, the ruler who knew his subordination to Yahweh, and who delayed the building of the temple that would serve in folk memory as the functional symbol of despotic royal power. He is the David whom the Deuteronomist lauded as the paragon of the king loyal to Yahweh. Given the possibility, however, that any reference to a king could be misunderstood, as indeed it has been, why does the oracle risk mentioning David at all? For several reasons. The tradition of which this oracle is an example regularly appeals to the ideal Davidide. The hope is that such a ruler will oppose elitist monarchist institutions and attitudes just as David opposed Nabal and Saul, and the Philistines and Arameans. Oracles of this type preempt the symbol of the ideal Davidide to forestall a counterappeal to a worse kind of Davidide in similar terms.

The image of the hut controls the figure of David rather than the other way around. That is, the monarchist glory of David is overshadowed by the humbleness of the hut. The effect is similar to displaying the Mona Lisa in the local train station: it would probably lose some of its aura. The hut is like a tent as opposed to a house (compare 2 Sam. 7:1–7). It is impermanent and contingent, and it represents dependency on Yahweh rather than self-sufficiency. Thus the Holiness Code preserves the interpretation that Israel lived in such huts during the exodus, when Israel was totally dependent on Yahweh (Lev. 23:43). They served as the RV's of the wasteland trek, analogous to God's movable tabernacle. The picture of the vineyard with its modest hut takes over in the remainder of the oracle, while the figure of David is left entirely undeveloped.

Is the vineyard a metaphor for a more ordinary Jerusalemite restoration? For the C editor, faintly, perhaps; for the original oracle, unlikely. This is no idyllic antiurban vision— it's too realistic for that. The cultivators of the new community will build *cities*. But they won't build *the* city. (*The* city, so to speak, is reduced to a hut.) No one city will control all the others. In a conspicuous omission, the cultivators build no towers in their cities nor walls around them. These props of monarchist power, typically built by enforced corvee for the benefit of the elite minority, the peasantry can do without. Citadels and walls are only good for the destruction prescribed in 1:3–2:5 (they are *singled out* in the C-stage oracles against Tyre, Edom, and Judah). The vineyards of the new community will be walled, but not the cities. The strength of the new cities lies in collective solidarity, the absence of monarchist power, and the protection of Yahweh.

The blessing of agricultural prosperity is prodigious:

> The plowman will come together with the reaper
> And the treader of grapes with the sower of seed
> And the mountains shall drip sweet wine
> And all the hills will melt with it.

Lev. 26:4–5 promises the blessing of a similar prosperity:

> I will give downpours to you in their proper season, and
> the earth will give its produce, and the tree of the field
> will give its fruit. Your threshing shall last to the time of
> vintage, and the vintage shall last to the time for sowing.

The last downpour occurs in the spring, before the threshing, and the first in the fall in time for plowing, just before sowing. Between these rains, according to this covenantal blessing, the threshing will reach to the vintage and the vintage to the sowing: thus the abundance spans the dry season. The second line in the Amos oracle, "the treader of grapes will come together with the sower of seed," may imply a more fundamental transition. It suggests a reversion to the pattern of land use in the hill country when egalitarian distributional land tenure obtained. Then small holders would devote their terraces and small plots to mixed farming, interspersing grain rows and garden plots among the vines and fruit trees, thus providing for all the essential needs of the clan on the spot. This pattern gave way, as we have seen, to the exclusive cultivation of single crops, usually vines or olive trees for commercial gain in the wake of latifundialization. Whether this oracle intends to allude to this specific form of land use or not, it foresees Yahweh expunging the land tenure patterns characteristic of the monarchic period. Its thrust is that the abundance will be withheld from the commercial sector to be consumed locally:

> They shall plant vineyards and *they* shall drink their wine
> They shall make orchards and *they* shall eat their fruit.

This oracle thus reverses oracles of the *A stage* in two different ways. At the A stage where it originates, it speaks to the peasantry and points to the new social structures—which are *old* as far as the peasantry are concerned—particularly land tenure, that are to replace the social structures doomed to annihilation. At the C stage, it is addressed in part to the Jerusalemite analogues and successors of the Samaritan ruling elite and portrays the abundance to be enjoyed by the new community of those who have said "The evil has gotten to me," of those who are fit for the new, just order.

The C-stage ending resolves the ambiguity and tension held in place by the B stage. The B-stage generation made the wrong choice. They are gone. The new, C-stage generation breaks through the suspended critical moment and enters fully into the festival of *succoth* with hope and confidence, inspired by its joy, endorsed by its blessing, and saved, not threatened, by God's appearance. The wheat has been threshed and refined (9:9), the booth is set up (9:11), and the wine vats are flowing (9:13). The remnant has been "gathered"—the same word is used for the ingathering of the summer fruits and the gathering of the remnant (compare Mic. 4:6–7; Zeph. 3:14–20; Jer. 6:9; 8:13). According to the Gezer Calendar, the appearance of the summer fruit (*qets*) marks the end (*qets*) of the agricultural year, while the "gathering" marks its new beginning. The C editor alludes to the same agricultural tradition to express his faith in this new beginning. The transition and its emotional impact have many similarities with the transition from pre-Advent to Advent and Christmas in the Christian liturgical year.

JUSTICE AND LIFE

Our theme has been that at all stages prophecy reveals God's justice. For the A and B stages, punishment and decision were the primary modes of this revelation. For the C editor, the primary data are his own survival and the circumstances of his existence which give him his hopeful outlook. The primary mode of his revelation of justice is life itself. The C editor only emphasizes what is, after all, the ground of justice whatever its manifestations, the ideal that life and its blessings are to be equally shared among all.

It is a paradox that the C-stage editor should be the one to come closest to the positive heart of the matter, the one to tell us about the *enjoyment* of God's justice. He is among the elite, like the B-stage editor. His work is even more learned, and in some ways less accessible, than the B stage. Its context is not simply the social one—his elite compeers—but to an even greater extent than with the B stage an intellectual and literary one, available to the very few. Who will hear his message of justice?

The paradox of the C stage—that it reveals the life-willing ground of God's justice only to the few—is a token of the paradox and potential tragedy of our own enjoyment of God's blessing, the pleasure of us few who read the C editor's work. Most of the readers of this book will be among the comparatively well-off in our society. We enjoy the life of 9:11–15, or at least seem to. At the same time it is highly questionable whether our life manifests God's justice as it should. In a world context, among all human beings, our kind of life is shared by only a few. We are far removed in space and time from the social catastrophes and miseries out of which God's justice raises people, so far indeed that the biblical symbols of distress, the symbols our tradition provides us for conceiving of our own past or present social hurt, grow pale and mute. I think this when people say to me, as they not infrequently do, "It's too bad we've lost the Psalms. There's a lot of material there we could use. They're a potentially rich resource." We talk about the Psalms, or the exodus, or the isolation of Abraham, with a dim nostalgia that suggests we are fast losing all "memory" of what the three-fourths of the world that hurts is really feeling. Needless to say we are far in spirit from the Torah story, the story behind all prophecy, that tells how the prosperity we enjoy is God-given, not self-acquired.

The one attitude fosters social justice, the other social hurt. It has proven very difficult for the blessed people of God to remember that since the justice of the blessed elite is very much in question, as in the B stage, their present blessing must be mostly a result of *God's* justice, not their own. Once across the Jordan, God's justice on our behalf becomes utterly contingent on our justice on others' behalf.

The C editor is freshly back in the land—even if only in imagination—filled with a consciousness of the contingency of his blessing and gladly embracing a vision of prosperity for the many in which his own social role may be dispensable. We sense the integrity of his faith and assent to the truth of his experience that God's justice is grounded in life. But *our* life, our prosperity, has a very different quality. American Christianity at virtually all levels pretends to be at the C stage. But every C stage evolves into a B stage. The challenge we face calls not for satisfied mutterings spilling out of hearts stupefied and mouths muffled by abundance, but for a deep awareness of the injustices we are part of and the ardent search for alternative actions and life-styles.

JONAH

The C editor deals with the reversal of Amos by composing into Amos B a quasi-logic of justice and mercy. Another way one could deal with the reversal of Amos—some will find it a more engaging way—would be to tell a story showing that, since to reject God's mercy is more absurd than to accept it, the only alternative is to accept it. This is the tack, and purpose, of the story of Jonah. Jonah is essentially a midrash on Amos C.

Jonah is indignant about God's habit of showing mercy. Admittedly there is a troublesome incongruity to · God's mercy, and it took some fancy literary footwork by the C-stage editor of Amos to make it intellectually satisfying. Still, everything else in the story of Jonah is turned on its head, too, and worse, leaving the reader little choice but to consider Jonah's anger to be as absurd as the rest and to accept God's mercy as the lesser absurdity.

Jonah is referred to only once outside the book of Jonah:

> [Jeroboam son of Joash] restored the territory of Israel from Lebo-Hamath to the Sea of the Arabah according to the word of Yahweh the God of Israel which he spoke through his servant Jonah son of Amittai the prophet from Gath-hepher. For Yahweh had seen the affliction of Israel as very instructive, there being neither retained nor released [no male—used as a curse against the dynasties of Jeroboam I and Omri], and no helper for Israel. Yahweh did not say he would blot out the name of Israel

from beneath the sky, so he delivered them through Jeroboam son of Joash (2 Kings 14:25–27).

Parts of this passage are difficult to translate, whether one's interests are historical, literary, or both. It says two things clearly, however: (1) Jonah prophesied in the reign of Jeroboam II (this is why Jonah comes just after Amos in the Bible, with only Obadiah coming in between as an elaboration on Amos 9:12), and (2) he prophesied victory instead of defeat. This passage suggests a prophetic debate between Amos and Jonah. Amos says Yahweh will blot out Israel; Jonah says Yahweh will save Israel. Jonah's positive counters Amos's negative.

In light of the book of Jonah, there seems to be a joke hidden here. How much midrashic interplay among this passage, Jonah, and Amos took place in their composition and transmission is unknown, though we have already identified an apparent connection between this passage and Amos 6:14. Vis-à-vis the passage in 2 Kings, the Jonah of the book of Jonah is incongruous: in the Kings passage he counters Amos's negative with a positive, whereas in the book of Jonah he counters the positive of God's mercy, which he himself represents in Kings, with a sullen negative. This is the first of the nonstop incongruities that make up the book of Jonah.

The story of Jonah is an uninterrupted chain of absurdities, one after another, from beginning to end. It has four scenes, corresponding to its four chapters, that produce a simple but important symmetry. The first and third scenes show Jonah among the heathen, the second and fourth Jonah with Yahweh. Let me review these four scenes and point out the more significant incongruities, many of which you will doubtlessly have noticed already in your reading of Jonah.

When Yahweh commissions Jonah to go east to Nineveh, without response Jonah goes west to Tarshish, paying his way to avoid Yahweh's command. He begins the descent that will take him all the way to Sheol because, as he insists at the very end, "It is good for me to be angry to death." Before anything has happened to him besides God's call, he wants to die.

"He *went down* to Joppa . . . and he *went down* into the ship
. . . and he *went down* into the far reaches of the hold . . .
and fell asleep (sounds like 'went down')." Then in his prayer
from the fish in scene two he concludes, "I *went down* into the
underworld." On the boat this prophet is the cause of distress
rather than its relief—which he might prefer, were it not for
its outcome—and he is the wrongdoer instead of the heathen.
Twice he jeopardizes their lives, once by being the target of
the tempest, again by having them throw him overboard and
risk shedding innocent blood. Despite the prophet in their
midst, the sailors are forced to cast lots to disclose the truth
about the tempest, and they must intercede for their own
innocent lives rather than the prophet doing it for them. The
heathen seem almost eager to be converted to the fear of
Yahweh: their "fear" (1:5) becomes "great fear" (1:10) and
then the "great fear of Yahweh" (1:16), and they hurriedly
sacrifice and make vows to their new God even though the
tempest had already abated. Quite despite himself, in a manner the opposite of the sailors' enthusiasm but in step with the
stages of their fear, Jonah serves as the agent of their conversion. He fearlessly falls asleep during the tempest (he is
ready to die—the sailors "fear"), he lies about his own "fear"
of Yahweh (he doesn't fear him at all—the sailors "fear with a
great fear" at Jonah's impiety), and he asks to be tossed into
the sea rather than make any redemptive display of "fear" on
his own behalf (the sailors "fear Yahweh with a great fear").

Fish don't swallow human beings whole. (I'm not saying the
story can't be fabulous; I am saying every element in it is
incongruous.) And human beings don't survive three days
inside fish. At last Jonah "cries out" (2:2), something he has
refused to do twice already (1:2,6). He does so when it is his
own isolated life at stake—he'll do what he can to save his own
life if he doesn't have to save others at the same time. Jonah
comes late to the piety of the heathen ("I will make sacrifice, I
will fulfill my vows"). Knowing that Jonah wants to die rather
than acknowledge God's mercy for others as just, we are surprised that he is so happy to acknowledge God's mercy for
himself: his prayer is more a prayer of confidence (Yahweh
has delivered me) than an appeal for help (Yahweh, deliver

me!), even though he is still in the fish. Jonah comes up as the fish's vomit, an undignifying, unenviable, and absurd rescue.

Yahweh commissions him again. Jonah heads off to Nineveh this time, to the "great city," where one could, as in the belly of the "great fish," spend three days. No sooner has Jonah set foot inside the gate of this wicked megalopolis than instantaneously there occurs "a truly convulsive" (J. A. Miles) response of repentance from king and people. Yet these are the Ninevites, the archvillains of the ancient world! The wording of Jonah's announcement, "Within forty days Nineveh will be *turned*," reminds the Hebrew reader unmistakably of Sodom and Gomorrah, which connote total depravity and incorrigible sinners without exception. Every reader of Jonah, from the first one on, has known that Nineveh can only postpone its destruction—it was expunged in 612 B.C.

Yet Jonah, desire as he might, cannot produce their end. His message, like Amos A's in the hands of the C editor, is too ambiguous, and there's nothing he can do about it. The word "turn" (not the same word as the Deuteronomistic cliche) can also mean a change of person or of heart, as with Saul in 1 Sam. 10:6, "you shall be turned into another man," and 10:9, "God turned his [heart] into another heart." Thus to Jonah's rage his proclamation unavoidably predicts Nineveh's change of heart as much as its downfall. Again despite himself, Jonah is about to be the agent of the heathens' conversion, even though he is commissioned, in the tradition of Amos A, to condemn them to death. Playing Amos A, Jonah is doomed to have his message heard the way Amos C hears Amos A. The Ninevites fulfill the prophecy the way Jonah didn't mean it, turning repentant from the top down, trusting (they aren't even certain, but have to have faith) that God would turn from the heat of his wrath. And so God does.

Thereby God produces in Jonah a worse burn than ever. In the fourth, as in the second scene, Jonah prays to Yahweh: "It is just as I've said all along: you are a patient, merciful God, so it's better for me to die than to live." What's Jonah's problem? His problem is that he doesn't like doing the business of a God who denounces people and then changes his mind. If God changes his mind, a prophet can't help being a false prophet. Why should Jonah condemn sinners to death if he knows God isn't going to follow through with the sentence? This, you see, is the C-stage question put in terms of Jonah's—or the A stage's—integrity, or, as Jonah's patronym (Amittai means "the true one") says, his truth. Where is the truth of prophecy if God can change his mind?

Jonah's prayer for death is like Elijah's in the wilderness (1 Kings 19:4), but Elijah was genuinely threatened by death on all sides, whereas Jonah has no one to fear but himself. As in 1 Kings 19, Yahweh imposes a two-stage interrogation: "Is it good for you to be hot (angry)?" Without answering, Jonah goes farther east (another act of defiance?) beyond the city, and sets up a gazebo (*succah*, as in the C-stage conclusion to Amos) to shade him from the heat. There, crouched facing west, he sullenly watches what's going on in the city, whispering to himself, we may imagine, Hebrew expletives. The gazebo, having no walls, is open at the back, where the sun will rise to make him "hot" the next morning. So Yahweh *appoints* a *vomit*-plant (a coined word—don't run to your botanical dictionary) to grow up fabulously fast and produce shade at the back of Jonah's head, to *deliver him* from his evil. The three italicized phrases connect the saving plant with the saving fish. Just as he was happy over the fish, so now, sitting all by himself again and thinking ahead to tomorrow morning with its rising sun behind his back, Jonah is happy about this plant appointed to keep him cool. But the plant never makes it through the night. In the morning Jonah is "hotter" than ever. Yahweh repeats his question: "Is it good for you to be hot because of the plant?" Jonah is consistent to the end: "It is good for me to be hot to death." Consistent, but wrong. "You have pity for the plant, which you did nothing for and which perishes in a night, and I should not have pity for Nineveh, which has over 120,000 obtuse people, and a lot of beasts?" The Ninevites are morally no more sophisticated than their cattle, but they did repent, and that's what matters.

The story is crazy from start to finish. And its finish is no resolution. It has no satisfying ending, as has long been felt.

The point of the story is not to take away Jonah's anger, but to caricature it, in order to show it for what it is. If it is a part of this crazy, crazy story, then it, too, must be crazy. Jonah wants to die, especially if he can't take the sinners with him. That's absurd. Jonah settles for God's mercy as long as it applies to him and no one else. That's absurd. Jonah expects God not to pity a myriad of human beings, but it's okay for Jonah to pity a single plant that's here today and gone tomorrow—and a lot less smart than the Ninevites, even if they are brutes. That's absurd. Jonah feels sorry for himself without ever feeling sorry for anyone else, even though he's no better than anyone else. That's the most absurd thing of all.

If Jonah's indignation is more absurd than God's mercy, then Amos C is possible—and maybe even necessary.

Recently a debate about whether the story of Jonah is supposed to produce a laugh or not scorched the pages of a well-known scholarly journal. It was an informative debate, but I'm relieved to think it basically doesn't matter, since attempts to get a laugh by retelling the story usually fall flat. If laughter is in essence a reaction to the humorous as the profoundly incongruous, then perhaps Jonah is meant to evoke laughter.

But the story is not simply funny. It spells the difference between life and death for its Judahite readers because it either establishes or fails to establish the credibility of God's mercy. The Ninevites are long dead. The Ninevites in the story are ultimately not themselves but the Judahite readers of Jonah, the ones who for the present have been delivered from Yahweh's sentence of death, if not by their conscious repentance, at least by their severe mortification in exile. The certainty of God's mercy, the very surety of their faith in themselves as God's people, depends on the success of the story of Jonah in making Jonah's indignation the greater absurdity. Whether one laughs with it or not, this is a deadly serious matter. If you *can* laugh at Jonah, at least you know you can share the joy of Amos C and at the same time feel certain that your roots are, temporarily, in the ground.

For Further Reading

A recent introduction to the development of the whole of
Old Testament literature from the perspective used in this
book is J. A. Sanders' excellent *Torah and Canon* (Philadelphia: Fortress Press, 1972). Two authors have dealt in detail
with the growth of prophecy: R. E. Clements, *Prophecy and
Tradition* (Atlanta: John Knox Press, 1975), and J. Blenkin-
sopp, *Prophecy and Canon* (Notre Dame: University of Notre
Dame Press, 1977). The entire January 1978 issue of *Interpretation* (Vol. 32, No. 1) is devoted to Old Testament prophecy; the bibliographical article by J. Limburg therein thoroughly covers the decade 1967–1977.

Those interested in hermeneutical issues raised by proph-
ecy may find the following helpful: J. A. Sanders, "Herme-
neutics," in *Interpreter's Dictionary of the Bible. Supplementary
Volume* (Nashville: Abingdon Press, 1976), pp. 402–7; R. L.
Rohrbaugh, *The Biblical Interpreter: An Agrarian Bible in an
Industrial Age* (Philadelphia: Fortress Press, 1977); and
W. Brueggemann, *The Prophetic Imagination* (Philadelphia:
Fortress Press, 1978).

The most recent and thorough commentaries on Amos are
J. L. Mays, *Amos: A Commentary* (Philadelphia: Westminster
Press, 1969), in the Old Testament Library series, and H. W.
Wolff, *Joel and Amos* (Philadelphia: Fortress Press, 1977), in
the Hermeneia series. Wolff takes an approach to Amos
much like the one in this book, and in more detail. A large
bibliography can also be found in his book. Wolff's *Amos the
Prophet* (Philadelphia: Fortress Press, 1973) represents an
earlier preliminary statement of Amos's setting. H. McKeat-
ing, *Amos, Hosea, and Micah* (New York: Cambridge Uni-

versity Press, 1971), in the New English Bible Commentaries series, is informative. The forthcoming commentary on Amos in the Anchor Bible (Garden City, N.Y.: Doubleday & Co., Inc.), by F. I. Andersen and D. N. Freedman, promises to be a worthwhile treatment.

The latest work on the formation of the book of Amos is the article by R. F. Melugin printed in *Seminar Papers. Society of Biblical Literature 1978*, Vol. 1 (Chico, Cal.: Scholars Press, 1978), pp. 369–91. Melugin reviews the hypotheses of H. W. Wolff and Klaus Koch (the latter not available in English), then gives his own detailed analysis of Amos 3–4.

Articles I have found particularly helpful in my preparation for this book include: J. de Waard, "The Chiastic Structure of Amos V 1–17," *Vetus Testamentum* 27 (1977), 170–77; R. Knierim, " 'I Will Not Cause It To Return' in Amos 1 and 2," in *Canon and Authority*, ed. G. W. Coats and B. O. Long (Philadelphia: Fortress Press, 1977), pp. 163–75; and G. W. Ramsey, "Speech-Forms in Hebrew Law and Prophetic Oracles," *Journal of Biblical Literature* 96 (1977) 45–58. H. H. Rowley's treatment of Amos 7 is contained in "Was Amos a Nabi?" *Festschrift* Otto Eissfeldt (Halle, 1947), pp. 191–98.

If you are interested in seeing how the perspective of this book might apply to a different prophetic book, try looking at J. L. Mays, *Micah: A Commentary* (Philadelphia: Westminster Press, 1976), in the Old Testament Library, or W. L. Holladay, *Isaiah: Scroll of Prophetic Heritage* (Grand Rapids: Wm. B. Eerdmans Publishing Co., 1978).

Those who want to find out more about the Deuteronomistic History will find it a pleasure to read W. E. Rast, *Joshua, Judges, Samuel, Kings* (Philadelphia: Fortress Press, 1978), in the Proclamation Commentaries series. The two editions of the Deuteronomist's work referred to in the present book are conveniently described in the chapter on "The Themes of the Book of Kings and the Structure of the Deuteronomistic History" in F. M. Cross, *Canaanite Myth and Hebrew Epic* (Cambridge, Mass.: Harvard University Press, 1973), pp. 274–89.

One of the important new developments in Old Testament studies is the growing interest in the sociology of agrarian societies and its bearing on ancient Israel. A start in this field can be made with G. and J. Lenski, *Human Societies. An Introduction to Macrosociology* (New York: McGraw-Hill Book Co., 1978, 3d ed.); E. R. Wolf, *Peasants* (Englewood Cliffs, N.J.: Prentice-Hall, Inc., 1966); and G. Sjoberg, *The Preindustrial City: Past and Present* (New York: Macmillan Publishing Co., Inc., 1960).

The following represent a selection from the increasing number of works applying sociological categories to the study of Israel. Next to the seminal works of G. E. Mendenhall (cited in the notes of most of the following), the works of Frick, Chaney, and Gottwald should be singled out. F. S. Frick's *The City in Ancient Israel* (Chico, Cal.: Scholars Press, 1977) provides an excellent overview of urban culture in ancient Israel. M. L. Chaney presents a balanced and readable account of the origins of early Israel in "Ancient Palestinian Peasant Movements and the Formation of Premonarchic Israel," *Biblical Archaeologist* (forthcoming). Immediately related to the subject of this book is M. A. Cohen, "The Prophets as Revolutionaries. A Sociopolitical Analysis," *Biblical Archaeology Review* May/June, 1979, 12–19. In this area of study, the works of N. K. Gottwald stand out. The following would be of particular interest to readers of this book: "Domain Assumptions and Societal Models in the Study of Premonarchic Israel," *Supplements to Vetus Testamentum* 28 (1975), 89–100; "Social and Economic Development of Israel," in *Interpreter's Dictionary of the Bible. Supplementary Volume* (Nashville: Abingdon Press, 1976), pp. 465–68; "Were the Early Israelites Pastoral Nomads?" *Biblical Archaeology Review* 4 (1978) 2–7; and *The Tribes of Yahweh: A Sociology of the Religion of Liberated Israel, 1250–1000 B.C.* (Maryknoll, N.Y.: Orbis Books, 1979). The problem of the origins of early Israel is debated from several angles in the May 1978 issue of *Journal for the Study of the Old Testament.*

A number of useful studies of Jonah have appeared recently: E. M. Good, "Jonah: The Absurdity of God," in *Irony in the Old Testament* (Philadelphia: Westminster Press, 1965), pp. 39–55; R. E. Clements, "The Purpose of the Book of Jonah," *Supplements to Vetus Testamentum* 28 (1975), 16–28; J. A. Miles, "Laughing at the Bible: Jonah as Parody," *Jewish*

Quarterly Review 65 (1975) 168–81; A. Berlin, "A Rejoinder to John A. Miles, Jr., With Some Observations on the Nature of Prophecy," *Jewish Quarterly Review* 66 (1976) 227–35; T. E. Fretheim, *The Message of Jonah. A Theological Commentary* (Minneapolis: Augsburg Publishing House, 1977); G. Lohfink, "Jonah and His God," in *The Bible—Now I Get It!* (Garden City, N.Y.: Doubleday & Co., Inc., 1979), pp. 78–84.

On the history and archaeology of Jerusalem during the monarchy, consult the summary of M. M. Eisman, "A Tale of Three Cities," *Biblical Archaeologist* 41 (1978) 47–60.

An excellent new study of the *marzech* is Marvin H. Pope, "Notes on the Rephaim Texts from Ugarit," *Essays of the Ancient Near East in Memory of J. J. Finkelstein* (Connecticut Academy of Arts and Sciences, Memoir 19), Hamden: Connecticut Academy of Arts and Sciences, 1977.

Ch. 1
prophetic spurts linked tog.
orig Amos — 3rd quarter, 8th c. Ⓐ before 722 B.C.
Ⓒ final comp - end of Baby ex. Ⓑ 7th C bet. Hezzekiah & Josiah
6th c.